OSPREY COMBAT AIRCRAFT • 73

B-26 MARAUDER UNITS OF THE MTO

SERIES EDITOR: TONY HOLMES

OSPREY COMBAT AIRCRAFT • 73

B-26 MARAUDER UNITS OF THE MTO

MARK STYLING

117 964

OSPREY
PUBLISHING

Front Cover
Capt Sidney 'Snuffy' Smith, CO of the 441st BS, led the 320th BG when it attacked the railway bridge at Rovereto, in Italy, on 21 January 1944. On the right wing of Smith's B-26C-45 42-107795 B/N 11 *Little Catherine* was B-26B-50 42-96016 B/N 04 *Doris K. – Iidalizeya*, flown by 1Lt Charles O'Mahony. The latter pilot recalled;

'Fighters intercepted our formation of 18 Marauders before the bomb run. "I've got fighters at 'one o'clock high!'" was the call that came crackling through my headphones. Definitely bad news, as we had no fighter escort, so these had to be bogeys. "Three at 'eleven o'clock level', two at 'twelve o'clock' and four at 'nine o'clock high!'" They were circling us like jackals, and with the same fighters being called in from different crew positions, it sounded like the whole Luftwaffe was there. With no urging, every ship in the formation pulled in closer to give us more concentrated firepower.

'Capt Smith's head looked like it was on a swivel as he tried to guess in which direction the fighters would make their first pass. Suddenly, his blue cap dropped from sight, and moments later his head reappeared, wearing a flak helmet. Things were getting serious.

'The air was glassy calm, and I had the wing of my ship well overlapped on the group lead. Then I saw dozens of parallel, ribbon-thin trails streaking under our aeroplanes. Christ – those trails are from machine gun shells! As fast as that dawned on me, the fighters hurtled by underneath us.

'The first pass was head-on from "12 o'clock high", as the fighters tried to knock out the lead ship. Our aeroplane's 0.50-cals were pounding in short bursts, and the bomber shuddered as it filled with acrid smoke and the smell of cordite. The chatter on the intercom was nonstop.

'After the first pass, the fighters formed into pairs and came at us from all directions. They closed on us until a midair seemed inevitable, then executed an abrupt half roll and split-essed down, leaving only their heavily armoured bellies as targets for our gunners. Two of our bombers drifted out of formation and headed down, trailing heavy smoke. No fighters followed them – obviously there was no need to. Both ships were going down. Our remaining aeroplanes bored steadily on while the fighters continued to gyrate all around us.

'Machine guns overheated and jammed, and my headset spouted obscenities from frustrated gunners. Both sides seemed to run out of ammunition at the same time. The fighters reassembled out of range and disappeared off to the northeast, in the direction of Austria. Once again, the only sound was the drone of our engines. We still had a bomb run to make, but at least there was no flak forecast.'

The two Marauders downed were B-26G-5 43-34396 B/N 01, flown by 2Lt Truman C Cole, and B-26C-45 42-107532 B/N 86, flown by 1Lt James N Logsdon. B-26G-5 43-34261 B/N 84, flown by 1Lt Charles W P Kaminski, which occupied the position to the left wing of the lead ship, was hit by flak on the bomb run and later ditched (*Cover artwork by Mark Postlethwaite*)

First published in Great Britain in 2008 by Osprey Publishing
Midland House, West Way, Botley, Oxford, OX2 0PH
443 Park Avenue South, New York, NY, 10016, USA
E-mail; info@ospreypublishing.com

ISBN: 978 1 84603 307 0

Edited by Tony Holmes
Page design by Tony Truscott
Cover Artwork by Mark Postlethwaite
Aircraft Profiles by Mark Styling
Index by Alan Thatcher
Originated by PDQ Digital Media Solutions
Printed and bound in China through Bookbuilders

ACKNOWLEDGEMENTS

The author would like to thank the following individuals for the provision of photographs published in this volume – Joe Baugher, Don Enlow, Pete Guerra, Jack Haher, Jim Hardy, Louise Hertenstein, Alf Egil Johannessen, Bruce Kwiatkowski, SSgt Roman S Kwiatkowski, Ronald Macklin, Si Ober, Chuck O'Mahony, Gust and Sophia Poplos, Franz Reisdorf and Lou Sykes.

CONTENTS

TRAINING AND EARLY COMBAT

In February 1941, the 17th Bombardment Group (Medium) gave the B-25 Mitchell – the USAAC's first modern twin-engined bomber – its frontline service debut. By September of that year, all four squadrons within the group had re-equipped with the aircraft. As the 17th became more proficient with the B-25, it was called upon to provide trained crews for the 38th, 42nd, 12th and 47th BGs that would duly operate A-20 Havocs, B-25 Mitchells and B-26 Marauders. The role the 17th played in establishing the Army Air Corps' medium bomber force led to it being dubbed the 'Daddy of Them All'.

Martin's B-26 Marauder was the newest of these American medium 'bombing twins', with the first examples having been issued to the USAAC in mid-1941. The 22nd BG was one of the earliest units to receive B-26s, and it was hastily sent to Australia in the aftermath of the Pearl Harbor raid on 7 December 1941. The group gave the bomber its combat debut in the South West Pacific Area (SWPA) on 5 April 1942, when B-26s sortied from Garbutt Field in Townsville, Queensland, and attacked the Japanese naval base at Rabaul, on New Britain.

Thirteen days later, the 17th BG provided the volunteer crews that conducted the audacious 'Doolittle Raid' on Japan. This extremely hazardous mission saw 16 B-25Bs launched from the aircraft carrier USS *Hornet* to bomb targets in the Japanese homeland.

In June 1942, the 17th and 21st BGs were selected as the two Operational Training Units (OTU) that would convert onto the B-26 Marauder in order to oversee the rapid creation of newly planned B-26 groups. The 17th BG duly moved from McChord Field, Washington, to Barksdale Field, Louisiana, whilst the 21st BG called MacDill, Florida, home. On 23 June, the latter group helped establish the 320th BG, and three days later the 319th BG was formed at Barksdale.

Once operating at full strength, both groups were comprised of four bombardment squadrons – the 319th BG controlled the 437th, 438th, 439th and 440th BSs, and the 320th BG oversaw the 441st, 442nd, 443rd and 444th BSs.

Crew training for these pioneer groups was blighted by problems, as early versions of Peyton Magruder's revolutionary design quickly garnered for themselves a reputation for being unforgiving if handled clumsily in the air. The root cause of most of these problems was the bomber's high wing loading, and this figure was steadily increased as production B-26s became heavier and heavier due the introduction of increased armament and protective crew armour. The combination of high wing loading and heavier weights meant that if a Marauder lost power on take-off it could not become airborne on just one engine.

A casualty of the 319th BG's move overseas, B-26B-2 41-17862 *"TIME'S AWASTIN"* of the 440th BS/319th BG became lost in the winter weather, ran out of fuel and force-landed in Labrador on 12 October 1942. Its crew (standing, left to right) consisted of pilot 1Lt Grover C Hodge Jr, co-pilot 2Lt Paul L Jannsen, (squatting, from left to right) gunner Sgt Bailey and radio operator Sgt Frank S Galm. Hodge, Jannsen and Galm, along with navigator 1Lt Emmanuel J Josephson, engineer Cpl Russell Reyrauch, gunner Cpl James J Mangini and passenger TSgt Charles Nolan, belly-landed near Saglek. They attempted to radio for help without success, and on 23 December, Jannsen, Josephson and Nolan took the life raft from the aeroplane and attempted to go for help, but were never seen again. Hodge knew from star shots that they were close to the Eskimo settlement of Hebron, but he believed it impossible to cross the mountains in the continuing bad weather. Their food supplies ran out on 17 January 1943, and the last entry was made in Hodge's diary on 3 February. Eskimos discovered the remaining four bodies with the aeroplane on 9 April 1943. It turned out that they were only 20 miles from Hebron (*Louise Hertenstein*)

High wing loading also meant high take-off speeds too, and if a B-26 lost power when accelerating down the runway, or shortly after rotating, it would almost inevitably crash because the pilot had insufficient power with one good engine to safely fly a circuit and land.

One of the primary causes of power failure on take-off in early B-26s was the malfunctioning of the electrical control system for the four-bladed 13 ft 6 in Curtiss Electric propellers fitted to the bomber. Such a failure would see the propeller run away uncontrollably, thus reducing the amount of power being cranked out by the affected engine.

Such problems were inevitable with a brand new aircraft that was being maintained by inadequately trained ground personnel and flown by inexperienced pilots in a wartime environment. Due to the frequency of these high-speed, often fatal, accidents, the B-26 quickly gained a poor reputation amongst crews that was reflected in nicknames such as the 'Flying Prostitute', 'Baltimore Whore' (both references to the B-26's short wingspan – i.e., no visible means of support – and city of origin), 'Flying Coffin' and 'Martin Murderer'. Two slogans of the period were 'One a day the Tampa way' and 'Two a day the Barksdale way'.

Increased training and technical modifications (a greater wing span to reduce wing loading, for example) to the B-26 helped, but the Marauder would never lose its reputation, despite it eventually having the lowest combat loss rate of all USAAF medium bomber types.

HEADING OVERSEAS

In late July 1942, the 17th, 319th and 320th BGs were selected to join the USAAF's Twelfth Air Force for the upcoming invasion of North Africa, code named Operation *Torch*, which was planned for early November 1942. The newly formed 335th BG relieved the 17th BG (which controlled the 34th, 37th, 95th and 432nd BSs) of its OTU status to enable the group to prepare for combat.

Training and expansion continued apace, and in September the groups prepared to move overseas. The 319th left first, with its ground echelon being ferried by sea whilst its new B-26Bs were flown to England via the North Atlantic Route – Maine to Greenland, then on to Iceland and finally to Prestwick, in Scotland. Overloading and bad weather took their toll, with two bombers disappearing without trace en route.

A third machine, B-26B-2 41-17862 *"TIME'S AWASTIN"* of the 440th BS, ran out of fuel on 12 October when its crew, led by pilot 1Lt Grover C Hodge Jr, became lost. He set the bomber down on Labrador, and when a rescue party had not arrived by the 23 December, three of the crew set off looking for help and were never seen again. The remainder, including Hodge (whose diary told the tale), eventually starved to death and were subsequently found with their aeroplane in April 1943.

B-26B-2 41-17790, flown by 2Lt Clarence Wall, was lured off course by false German radio beacons and missed Scotland entirely! It crash-landed at Noord Beveland, on the Dutch coast, thereby placing a flyable example of the hitherto unknown type in the hands of the Germans.

Once in the UK, the 319th headed to England in preparation for the long flight to North Africa. Yet more losses were suffered during the journey from England to North Africa due to crews' inexperience when it came to bad weather flying. The group set out for Algeria on 12 November, and

B-26B-2 41-17751 *SNAFU*, flown by 'Doolittle Raid' pilot Capt Donald G Smith, hit a hill near Huntington, in Yorkshire, and its crew perished. Later that same day, group CO Lt Col Alvin G Rutherford was aboard one of two 439th BS B-26s (41-17774 *The Hobo*, flown by Capt Frank Tuttle, and 41-17777 *Boogie Woogie*, flown by William A Bloom Jr) that became lost in bad weather, strayed over the Cherbourg peninsular and were probably shot down by flak.

Four days prior to these losses, the group's ground echelon had gone ashore with the *Torch* force, landing at Arzeu beach, in Algeria. With the Allies firmly established in North Africa, the surviving B-26s headed south during mid-November. When the group finally reached its new home at Maison Blanche airfield, near Algiers, it had only 17 serviceable Marauders on strength of the 57 that had been despatched from the USA!

Despite these hardships, the 319th BG flew its first combat mission from Telergma on 28 November, when B-26s were sent to bomb Kairouan airfield in Tunisia. Maj David M Jones, who had received the Distinguished Flying Cross (DFC) following his participation in the 'Doolittle Raid', led the nine B-26s. Seeing no worthwhile targets at Kairouan, the crews flew on to the port of Sfax, where they dropped 69 300-lb bombs from 1000 ft. They made multiple runs on port installations and used their defensive armament for ground strafing – B-26B-2s were not equipped with the package guns that were subsequently fitted to all frontline variants from the B-10 onward.

The only casualty suffered by the group was a tail gunner wounded by flak, and all bombers returned to base. Such low-level attacks soon proved to be costly, however, and losses began to mount. The crews had been trained to conduct low-level bombing using the D-8 bombsight, and they would continue to do so for a month before losses became too prohibitive.

On 30 November nine B-26s, escorted by USAAF P-38s, attacked the Axis airfield at Gabes, in Tunisia. This time the flak was accurate, and B-26B-2 41-17754 *SUSFU*, flown by 1Lt David L Floeter of the 439th BS, crash-landed in the desert. The crew quickly set the wreckage of their Marauder alight, before being rescued by a 15th BS A-20 Havoc. The B-26 flown by 1Lt Ashley Woolridge returned to base with a severely wounded tail gunner, and when Sgt Robert L Christman died five days later, he became the unit's first confirmed combat fatality.

Al Aouina airfield was attacked on 2 December by the 319th BG, with many of the 12 B-26s sortied again receiving flak damage – one crash-landed upon its return to base. Forty-eight hours later, Maj Jones (in B-26B-2 41-17815) led six Marauders against shipping in Bizerte harbour. Intense flak was encountered, and two aircraft were lost, including the bomber flown by Maj Jones. Aboard his B-26 was new group CO Lt Col Sam Agee, who had only arrived at Maison Blanche the previous evening. Jones force-landed and the crew became PoWs – Agee later escaped and spent the rest of the war in the Pentagon.

On leaving the target area, the formation, and its eight P-38 escorts from the 71st FS/1st FG, was attacked by both Fw 190s and Bf 109s. A gunner aboard one of the Marauders claimed a Messerschmitt destroyed.

Three more missions were flown from Maison Blanche before the group moved to Telergma, located in the Rhumel River valley in the Algerian mountains. Unlike Maison Blanche, which was an established pre-war airfield, Telergma was simply a dirt strip hastily constructed by army engineers. Most air- and groundcrew lived in tents, although senior personnel were quartered in a nearby village. Conditions were primitive at best, as there were few airfield facilities, and routine maintenance had to be conducted in the open. Persistent winter rain quickly turned the base to mud, making conditions difficult for men and machinery alike.

The 319th BG flew its first mission from Telergma on 15 December, when it attacked the coastal town of Sousse. Despite being opposed by accurate flak, the group dropped its ordnance from between 600 ft and 1000 ft. However, 437th BS B-26B-2 41-17759 *Horsefeathers*, flown by Capt Ellis E Arnold, was hit several times during its bombing run and crashed in the Gulf of Tunis. The CO of XII Bomber Command (which controlled all USAAF bomber assets in-theatre), Col Charles T Phillips, was part of Arnold's crew – no one survived the crash.

Some 48 years later, the wreckage of 41-17759 was discovered during dredging in the Gulf of Tunis. The remains of the bomber's crew – Arnold, Phillips, 1Lt Robert B Jenkins and Sgts John R Brdeja, Joseph Johnson Jr and Maurice L Cohen – were removed from the aircraft and finally laid to rest at Arlington National Cemetery on 23 April 2003.

On 17 December 1942, five B-26s conducted the first maritime patrol (sea sweep) north of the Gulf of Tunis. No Axis merchant ships were found, but a Ju 88 was shot down by a 439th BS aircraft flown by 1Lt Edward H Gibbs. The next day, five Marauders from the 438th and 439th BSs joined six B-25s from the 310th BG in an attack on the Sousse railway marshalling yards. Running in at between 800 ft and 1200 ft, the B-26s dropped their ordnance, but 41-17766 *I Dood It*, flown by 1Lt Gibbs, was hit by flak and exploded over the target. 438th BS B-26B-2 41-17803, flown by 1Lt Charles J Leonard, was also shot down into the nearby harbour. There were no survivors from either crew. The remaining three B-26s were also hit by flak, but they made it back to base.

The low-level medium bomber missions flown during December showed a loss rate of 8.2 per cent, and as a result, the commander-in-chief of the Twelfth Air Force, Brig Gen James H Doolittle, ordered that all future missions against land targets be conducted at medium altitudes (around 10,000 ft) using the Norden bombsight.

Although barred from attacking land-based targets at low-level, 319th BG crews began receiving training in the art of skip-bombing maritime targets from 28 December. Such attacks would see B-26s approaching their targets at heights of just 200 ft or less. When the group carried out these missions, if no suitable target could be found, crews tried to attack alternate land targets at the same altitude, thus contravening Doolittle's orders. Attacks on ships utilised both 500-lb bombs and British 325-lb depth charges. Some crews also received training in the employment of torpedoes, but no Twelfth Air Force groups used this weapon in anger.

Bombs were dropped using a modified N-6 reflector gunsight taken from the Bell top turret and relocated ahead of the co-pilot. A number of freighters and barges were sunk, but flak continued to take its toll.

17th BG INTO ACTION

Due to the worsening winter weather, it was decided that both the 17th and 320th BGs would head to North Africa via the newly established South

Atlantic route. The B-26B-2s of the 17th left first, staging through Puerto Rico, British Guinea and Brazil, before tackling the long overwater flight to Ascension Island and then continuing on to the Gold Coast. The group finally arrived at its new home at Telergma, in Algeria, on 23 December 1942, whereupon it joined up with the 319th BG, which had flown in from Maison Blanche a little over a week earlier.

On 30 December the 17th BG entered combat when the group sent six B-26Bs to bomb Gabes airfield. The unit had arrived in North Africa with one in four of its Marauders equipped with a Norden bombsight, and this vital piece of equipment allowed the aircraft to hit targets from altitudes above the enemy's flak envelope with just as much accuracy as if they had made their attack at 600 ft.

The B-26s encountered both flak and fighters over Gabes, and all but one of them sustained damage. Indeed, two Marauders were so badly shot up by Bf 109Gs from JG 53 that they belly landed upon their return to Telergma. The 17th BG sent 12 more Marauders to bomb Gabes on New Year's Eve, and this time the aircraft were escorted by ten P-40Fs from the 33rd TFS. The group suffered its first loss when B-26B-2 41-17905 (flown by 1Lt Phillip W Bailey) of the 432nd BS was hit by flak over the target area, forcing it to lag behind the formation. The Marauder was then set upon by German fighters and quickly shot down, with the loss of its entire crew.

For the next month the 17th BG attacked Axis airfields and transport routes, as well as joining the 319th BG in a series of anti-shipping missions – part of the Twelfth Air Force's campaign to stop supplies from Sicily reaching Axis forces in North Africa. During this period, the 319th BG's serviceability rates dropped to just six B-26s, so XII Bomber Command ordered the recently arrived 320th BG to transfer 18 aeroplanes and six crews to the beleaguered group.

Elements of the 320th began reaching the group's new base at Tafaraoui, 400 miles east of Oran, on 22 November 1942 following their transatlantic crossing. The last flight arrived in Algeria on 2 January 1943. Having then given most of its B-26Bs to the 319th BG, the group began training in medium level tactics prior to entering combat.

On 7 February the 17th BG participated in the Twelfth Air Force's first raid on a European target when it sent 19 Marauders to attack the Cagliari-Elmas airfield complex on the Italian island of Sardinia. Six days later, the group joined forces with the 319th BG to send 25 B-26s to bomb El Aouina airfield once again. Twelve Marauders returned early due to bad weather, and the rest lost their fighter escort and were attacked by II./JG 2. One B-26 was shot down over the target area and a second bomber crash-landed in Allied territory.

The 319th BG was withdrawn from combat on 15 February and sent to retrain and re-equip. The group handed over its last 17 Marauders to the 17th BG, which was now the only operational B-26 unit in the Twelfth Air Force, as the 320th BG was still not ready to enter combat.

On 17 February, the 17th BG joined other groups flying B-17s and B-25s for a series of raids on the Sardinian airfield at Decimomannu. Some 17 Marauders were despatched, and B-26B-2s 41-17839 *Air Corpse*, flown by Capt Frank K Walsh of the 95th BS, and 41-17850, flown by 2Lt Ernest F Case of the 432nd BS, collided over the target area.

B-26B 41-17829 *ARLEEN* of the 432nd BS was one of the original Marauders assigned to the 17th BG, the bomber subsequently being ferried to the MTO by Capt Charles H Diamond and his crew. Promoted to major and made CO of the 95th BS, Diamond was lost on 16 July 1943 when his B-26B-10 (41-18193 *Junior*) was shot down over Naples' central railway marshalling yard. The bomber crashed near Mt Vesuvius after the crew had baled out to become PoWs. *ARLEEN* lasted longer than its original crew, however, going on to complete 65 missions before being passed to the Free French Air Force (*Bruce Kwiatkowski*)

Exactly one week later, the 17th BG targeted El Aouina once more. Despite being escorted by Spitfire VBs from the USAAF's 52nd FG, the bombers were set upon by Bf 109Gs from II./JG 53 and three 37th BS aircraft shot down – these machines may have also been hit by the intense flak barrage thrown up over the target area. The aircraft lost were B-26B-2s 41-17868, flown by 1Lt Henry C Schmelig Jr, 41-17873, flown by 1Lt Harry T Martin, and 41-17912 *Pardon Me*, flown by 1Lt Lester D Rowher. Ten other Marauders were damaged by flak, including 41-17916 *NEW YORK CENTRAL*, flown by Capt Garnet Dilworth. This aeroplane was salvaged after crash-landing at Telergma with mortally wounded turret gunner SSgt Albert L Dalton on board.

1 March saw yet more losses suffered by the 17th BG as it bombed road and railway bridges at La Hencha, between Gabes and Sfax. These well-defended bridges were part of a major supply route for General Erwin Rommel's *Afrika Korps*, and XII Bomber Command gave the 17th four days to destroy them from either high or low altitude.

Eight Bf 109Gs from II./JG 77 succeeded in penetrating the P-38 fighter screen put up by the 82nd FG and quickly shot down 95th BS B-26B-2 41-17898 *Barrel House Bessie*, flown by 1Lt Hiram F Appleget, northwest of Kasserine Pass. Minutes later, 432nd BS B-26B-2 41-17928 *Terrible Terrapin*, flown by Capt Allan E Karstens, also went down in flames over the target.

B-26B-2 41-17858 *COUGHIN' COFFIN*, flown by Capt William R Pritchard, was badly damaged by flak during the raid. Its pilot had given the bomber its distinctive nickname due to its misfiring engines, which had plagued the aircraft during its ferry flight to North Africa. Attacking the bridges from an altitude of just 60 ft, the Marauder actually scraped the ground at one point and only just avoided crashing when it was rocked by the concussion of nearby bomb blasts. The crew dropped its bombs on the railway bridge and completed the 100-mile return journey across enemy territory at treetop height, earning Pritchard the DFC.

On 11 and 24 March, the 17th BG tried its hand at skip-bombing, and lost a single aircraft on both dates as the group attacked Axis shipping in the Mediterranean. The 432nd BS's 41-17914 *Defiant*, flown by 2Lt Daniel C Logan, was shot down by an Me 210 from III./ZG 1 whilst targeting Siebel ferries on the 11th, and 41-17883, flown by 2Lt Robert

Photographed at Djedeida, in Tunisia, in the autumn of 1943, B-26B-2 41-17858 *COUGHIN' COFFIN* was named and regularly flown by Capt William R Pritchard. On 11 July 1943 it became only the second 17th BG Marauder to reach the 50-mission mark. 1Lt Fred Meher flew the aeroplane on its final mission, in late October 1943, with Pritchard tagging along as an observer. The bomber was then sent back to the US, having been designated combat weary. The 34th BS's Thunderbird emblem adorned the starboard side of the bomber's nose, and the names of Pritchard's original crew appeared beneath the co-pilot's window (*Bruce Kwiatkowski*)

The head of pilot 2Lt Franklin P Bedford can be seen in the astrodome of his bomber (B-26B 41-17747 *Earthquake McGoon* of the 37th BS/17th BG) as he surveys damage inflicted by a direct hit from an 88 mm shell on the port engine nacelle. The Marauder had been hit whilst on its bomb run against La Smala airfield on 24 March 1943. The pilot carried on with his attack, dropping his bombs and then returning to Telergma and crash-landing. Just visible under the rear fuselage of the aircraft is the 'tunnel' machine gun, fitted to the rear crew entry hatch. This defensive position was subsequently deleted by Martin on its production lines when guns were fitted to the waist windows instead. *Earthquake McGoon* has been field modified with two guns in the latter position as well (*Author*)

Right
B-26B-3 41-17964 *"SAY UNCLE"* of the 442nd BS/320th BG lifts off at the very end of the runway at Montiescquieu. Starting with the B-4 model, Marauders were fitted with a longer nose wheel strut to help reduce the type's notoriously long take-off run. The resulting bulge added to the nose wheel doors is therefore missing from this B-3 model. The letter 'A' on the rear fuselage was the 320th BG's first method of individual aircraft identification. The running duck nose art was applied to many of the early Marauders flown in combat in North Africa by the 442nd BS. Note the lone Swordfish parked behind the bomber (*via Franz Reisdorf*)

W Grey of the 37th BS, was hit by flak and crashed with a wing on fire near Cape Bizerte on the 24th.

The day after the first skip-bombing mission, the 17th BG despatched 15 B-26s to attack the road/railway bridge east of Enfidaville, in Tunisia. B-26B-2 41-17840 *Glory Bound*, flown by 2Lt Harry F Pardee of the 432nd BS, was shot down by a Bf 109 prior to reaching the target, although the remaining B-26s succeeded in dropping 500-lb demolition bombs from 5000 ft. A number of near misses on the bridge were recorded, and an adjacent supply dump was hit.

Aside from skip-bombing Axis shipping on 24 March, the 17th BG also attacked La Smala airfield on the east coast of Tunisia. 37th BS B-26B-2 41-17747 *Earthquake McGoon*, flown by 1Lt Frank P Bedford, was hit by flak during its bomb run, an 88 mm shell tearing into its engine nacelle and exploding. Turret gunner TSgt Robert Rapp, who could see the extent of the damage, notified the pilot, who pressed on to the target area at the request of his wounded bombardier, 2Lt Harwood Means. The B-26 then limped back to base as slowly as possible due to the severe vibration caused by the flak damage. The crew was forced to jettison as much equipment as possible to allow the pilot to perform a belly landing at Telergma, as the bomber's hydraulic system had been shot out.

Two weeks of poor weather then brought a halt to missions for the 17th BG until 10 April, when the group attacked bridges and airfields in the Cap Bon Peninsula.

320th BG ENTER THE FRAY

In early February the 320th BG finally commenced combat operations when it began flying anti-submarine patrols off the coast of North Africa. The unit met with immediate success, claiming the destruction of a U-boat on the 12th of the month – no vessels were listed as lost by the *Kriegsmarine* on this date, however.

The unit moved from Tafaraoui to Montiescquieu, in Algeria, shortly afterwards, and it was from here that the 320th carried out its first land bombing mission on 22 April. Escorted by P-40s of the 325th FG, 18 Marauders, led by Capt Theodore M Dorman of the 444th BS in B-26B-2 41-17959 *Miss Fortune*, bombed Carloforte harbour, on Sardinia. The aircraft dropped both 100-lb and 300-lb bombs from an altitude of 8700-7700 ft, encountering only inaccurate flak. All the B-26s returned safely.

By this time Axis forces were steadily retreating towards their last toehold in North Africa – the Cap Bon Peninsula. As German and Italian troops pulled back, the 17th and 320th BGs kept the pressure on them by attacking ports and airfields on the Tunisian coast, as well possible destinations for retreating forces on Sardinia. A mission to the Italian island on 23 April saw 18 320th BG bombers target the port of Arbatax. Some 22 P-38s from the 82nd FG again provided fighter escort for the Marauders, but Bf 109Gs succeeded in getting through to the bombers and shooting up 442nd BS B-26B-2 41-17865 *Fuzzy Baby*, flown by squadron CO Capt Gordon F Friday. The Marauder was written off in a crash-landing at Cape Rosa, becoming the group's first combat loss in the process.

During that same mission, 1Lt Carl E Hoy of the 441st BS was awarded the group's first DFC for returning the heavily damaged

41-17776 *Most Likely* to base, whilst the first aerial victory was claimed by SSgt Martin E Furrer, bombardier aboard 41-18092 *Dorothy II*, flown by 1Lt Marshall W Doxse.

On 25 April the 320th was scheduled to attack Milis airfield, on Sardinia, but it aborted the mission when the fighter escorts failed to materialise. XII Bomber Command had ordered that no more un-escorted missions were to be attempted following the Arbatax raid. A Marauder was still lost, however, when parafrag (parachute retarded fragmentation) bombs ignited in the bomb-bay of 442nd BS B-26B-2 41-17965, flown by 1Lt Hardie R Tatum. The aircraft crashed into the sea and there were no survivors.

The following day, the 320th attacked the Sardinian town of Porto Ponte Romano, but all the bombs dropped missed their target. On 28 April the group was scheduled to go to Mabtouha landing grounds, in Tunisia, but weather intervened, forcing them to attack shipping off Cap Bon instead. Intense and accurate flak claimed three B-26B-2s – 41-18040, flown by Capt Richard L Chick of the 444th BS, ditched in the sea off Sousse, while 443rd BS B-26B-2s 41-18073, flown by 1Lt Thomas Summers, and 41-18059 *Big Butch*, flown by Capt James H Luttrell, crash-landed behind Allied lines.

On 29 April, the mission to Sidi Athma landing grounds, again in Tunisia, was aborted when escorting fighters failed to show up. The 320th then flew sea sweeps between 1 and 8 May, before participating in a large strike on the Sicilian city of Palermo on the 9th. A total of 211 Allied aircraft took part in this mission, with the 320th BG despatching 37

B-26B-3 41-17959 *Miss Fortune*, flown by Capt Theodore M Dorman of the 444th BS, led the 320th BG's first mission against a land-bsed target – Carloforte harbour, on Sardinia – on 22 April 1943. It is seen here taxiing in at Montiescquieu airfield, in Algeria, at the end of a mission in the early spring of 1943. Clearly visible beneath its fuselage is the mounting for a Mk 13 torpedo. Marauders had used this weapon in combat in the Southwest Pacific and Aleutian campaigns, although it is doubtful that any targets were ever hit with the torpedo. At that time the Mk 13 was a notoriously unreliable weapon, and the B-26 had proven itself to be vulnerable to flak when launching a torpedo attack. Operational trials were carried out in North Africa, but skip bombing was quickly developed as an alternative method for attacking surface ships. *Miss Fortune* also has package guns retrofitted, this additional armament being added to production aircraft from the B-10 and C-5 models onward (*via Franz Reisdorf*)

"SAY UNCLE" was assigned to 1Lt Rudy Morley, and its crew chief was TSgt Douglas M Boteler. The 442nd BS pilots posing here for the camera are (from left to right) 1Lts Harry A Holmes, Marsh Doxee, Wayne Church and Aram Otto Bayramian (*via Franz Reisdorf*)

Below and bottom
B-26B-4 41-18017 *DEVIL'S PLAYMATE*, assigned to the 442nd BS/320th BG, displays an interesting, and as yet unexplained, marking consisting of yellow and red bands on the tail gunner's fairing. These were possibly used as a lead ship identifier for other crews when in flight. The bomber's assigned pilot was 1Lt Harry A Holmes (*via Franz Reisdorf*)

B-26s and the 17th BG 18 aeroplanes. The 320th lost B-26B-2 41-17768 of the 442nd BS, flown by Capt Davis B Elliott, when it caught fire after being hit by flak and crashed into the sea near St Vith.

Another joint effort was conducted on the 11th, when seven waves of bombers devastated the Sicilian port of Marsala. 320th BG gunners claimed three Axis fighters destroyed whilst dropping their ordnance on railway marshalling yards, warehouses and shipping in the harbour.

The 17th BG then moved to its new base at Sedrata, in the Souk Ahras Province of Algeria, which brought the group closer to its assigned targets in Italy's Mediterranean islands. Several days later, on 13 May, the last German and Italian units in North Africa finally surrendered.

Having helped knock out the *Afrika Korps*, the 17th and 320th BGs now focused their efforts on Sardinia, bombing the railway marshalling yards at Cagliari and Porto Ponte Romano on 13 and 14 May.

ISLAND ATTACKS

Having defeated Axis forces in North Africa, the Allies now turned their attentions to the Mediterranean islands of Sardinia and Sicily as a prelude to the invasion of Italy itself. As mentioned in the previous chapter, the 17th BG moved to an airfield near the Algerian town of Sedrata, close to the border with Tunisia, in early May in preparation for the island bombing campaign that was to keep the Twelfth Air Force occupied throughout the summer of 1943.

Like most airstrips in Algeria, Sedrata was a hot, dusty, desert base that had been hastily constructed by US Army engineers just weeks prior to its occupation. The dust caused endless maintenance problems that added to the groundcrews' burgeoning workload, as they tried to prevent mechanical failures from downing bombers over the Mediterranean.

The 17th BG flew its first mission from Sedrata on 18 May, when it joined the 320th in a raid on Pantelleria. This 42-square-mile volcanic island lies in the Strait of Sicily 62 miles southwest of Sicily itself and 43 miles east of the Tunisian coast. The island was a strategically important base from which Axis aircraft could attack Allied shipping sailing along the North African coast. It was also viewed by senior Allied commanders as key territory that had to be taken prior to the planned invasion of Sicily.

Supreme Commander of the Allied forces in Europe Gen Dwight D Eisenhower duly directed Lt Gen Carl A Spaatz, commander of Northwest African Air Forces, to use concentrated heavy bombing to neutralise Pantelleria's defences – a 10,000-strong garrison of Axis troops – to such an extent that an invasion could not be contested.

As ordered, between 8 May and 11 June, Allied aircraft (primarily from the Twelfth Air Force) dropped 6313 tons of bombs on Pantelleria during a campaign code named Operation *Corkscrew*. On 11 June a white flag was raised on the island's airfield just before the first wave of British troops came ashore, and almost immediately the garrison surrendered. Eisenhower was proved right in his belief that air power alone could be used almost exclusively in certain circumstances to bring about victory without the involvement of ground forces. The example of Pantelleria would greatly influence subsequent Allied plans during World War 2.

As well as taking part in *Corkscrew*, the 17th and 320th BGs continued to bomb Sardinia and Sicily too. Indeed, the latter group attacked Decimomannu airfield three days running on 19, 20 and 21 May. During each of these missions, escorting P-40s managed to keep defending fighters at bay, and no B-26s were shot down.

With operational conditions as harsh as they were, however, casualties were inevitable, and on 23 May the 320th BG lost its CO when Lt Col John Fordyce crashed in 441st BS B-26B-2 41-18035 *Lady Kay III*. The four-man crew had been en route to 47th BW (the wing that controlled all B-26 operations in North Africa) HQ when the crash occurred – no one survived the accident. The group's base at Montiescquieu would later be renamed in Fordyce's honour.

B-26B-2 41-17765 *"LADY HALITOSIS"* of the 441st BS/320th BG flew 43 missions before being selected to return to the US for promotional duties on 15 July 1943. The artwork appeared on both sides of the bomber's nose, which by mid-July also sported the second version of the 441st BS insignia. This version had the central scroll and motto positioned at more of an angle across the silhouette of the USA. The scroll incorporated the squadron motto *'Finis Origine Pendet'* ('The end depends upon the beginning'), which was a quotation taken from the astrological poem Astronomica of Manilius, written by Roman poet Marcus Manilius (*via Franz Reisdorf*)

The crew of *"LADY HALITOSIS"* pose for the camera. They are (from left to right), John N McVay, Lamar S Timmons, Barclay P Malsbury, Robert A Marco and Luther W Greenlee (*via Franz Reisdorf*)

That same day, the 319th BG took delivery of 45 new B-26B-10s and identical B-26C-10s (the latter built in Martin's Omaha, Nebraska, facility), which boasted an increased wingspan of 71 ft and a vertical tail that was also taller and larger in area. Although these modifications increased the weight of the aircraft, they reduced the wing loading, therefore improving the handling characteristics of the Marauder when taking off and landing.

The B-26B-10's larger tail area led to the 319th BG being dubbed 'The Big-Assed Birds'. The 17th BG was nicknamed 'Daddy of Them All' (a reference to its earlier OTU status), whilst the 320th BG would start to be called 'The Boomerangs' from early 1944 due to the group's low loss rate.

The 17th BG, led by Maj Ross Greening, bombed the Sardinian transport base at Alghero on 24 May, destroying hangars and a fuel storage dump without loss. The following day the 320th BG attacked Porto Empedocle, on Sicily. B-26B-2 41-17859 of the 442nd BS, flown by 2Lt William E Osborn, left formation for unknown reasons during the mission and was not heard from again. B-26B-2 41-17765 *"LADY HALITOSIS"*, flown by 1Lt John N McVay, returned early, having had its bombs drop through the still closed bomb-bay doors.

Decimomannu was attacked once again on 27 May, and the 320th met with heavy opposition – eight B-26s were damaged either by flak or fighters, but none were lost. The following day the group bombed Milo airfield, near Trapani, on Sicily. The only loss suffered was B-26B-2 41-17981 *The Shark*, flown by 2Lt John B Stumm, which had gear problems caused by flak damage and was salvaged following a crash-landing upon its return to Montiescquieu.

The 17th BG attacked Castel Vetrano airfield that same day, and B-26B-2 41-17884 *Uncle Sam's Peace Terms* crashed on take-off, whilst flak damaged 41-17852 *Bronco* was written off in a belly landing when it returned to Sedrata.

On 1 June the 320th BG again bombed Porto Ponte Romano, after which B-26B-2 41-17851, flown by 1Lt John H Barber, crash-landed at Bon and was declared a total loss.

The 319th BG also returned to combat on 1 June when it joined the 17th BG at Sedrata. All three B-26 groups, and the P-40-equipped 325th FG, were then transferred from the 47th BW to the newly formed 2686th Provisional Wing.

The 319th flew its first mission from Sedrata to Porto Ponte Romano on 5 June, after which it completed

eight *Corkscrew* missions through to the 11th. On the latter date, the 319th's target was changed at the last minute due to the surrender of Pantelleria, and it sent bombers to the island of Lampedusa (off the North African coast) instead. 437th BS B-26C-10 41-34870, flown by 2Lt Thomas T Johnson, was damaged over the target by AAA and crashed near Le Kef. The crew baled out, but

Johnson was killed when his parachute failed to open. The garrison on Lampedusa surrendered the next day.

During the latter part of June through to mid July, all three groups continued to attack airfields on Sardinia and Sicily – Milo, Bo Rizzo, Milis, Castel Vetrano, Capoterra, Decimomannu, Carcitella and Gerbini were amongst those regularly bombed. Such missions allowed the Twelfth Air Force to reduce the effectiveness of both the Luftwaffe and the *Regia Aeronautica* prior to the forthcoming invasion of Sicily, code named Operation *Husky*. Despite being outnumbered, Axis fighters continued to defend these airfields. Flak also claimed its victims too.

On 15 June, 320th BG B-26B-2 41-17724 *RED HOT*, flown by 1Lt John Stumm of the 444th BS, was hit by flak over Milo. The bomber limped back to Montiescquieu and landed on one wheel and without brakes. The left engine was torn from its mount in the crash and *RED HOT* was salvaged. None of the crew suffered any injuries, however. This was Stumm's second crash in three weeks following a raid on Milo.

Other targets were hit as well, with both the 319th and 320th BGs attacking the Sicilian port of Olbia on the 18th. The latter group suffered no losses, but three Marauders from the 319th were destroyed. The mission had started badly when 2Lt Harold Mesco's B-26B-10 41-18301 *Dodo Bird II* of the 437th BS crashed on take-off at Sedatra.

Twelfth Air Force B-25s had attacked Olbia just prior to the 36 B-26s arriving over Sicily, so the port's defences were fully alert. The flak was intense, and Bf 109Gs and Macchi C.202s also attacked the formation. Flak claimed 437th BS B-26B-15 41-31603 *Our Baby*, flown by 1Lt Roger L Zeller – the bomber went down in the target area, and two parachutes were seen. The next victim was 438th BS B-26B-10 41-18318, flown by Capt John B Beard, which was lost shortly afterwards. Upon leaving the target area, the bombers were again set upon by fighters, and flak-damaged 437th BS B-26B-10 41-18291, flown by 1Lt James Schoonover, went down, chased by a Bf 109G. Its six-man crew parachuted into the sea.

B-26B-2 41-17724 *RED HOT* was destroyed in a crash-landing at Montiescquieu following a mission to Milo airfield on 15 June 1943. The bomber came to grief when it careered into an irrigation ditch that ripped off its starboard engine. Note that the B-26 still has the yellow surround to its national insignia, this marking having applied as a recognition aid for the *Torch* landings (*via Franz Reisdorf*)

RED HOT was adorned with nose art incorporating the 444th BS 'rabbit' emblem that was applied to many of the squadron's early Marauders. The bomber is seen here with its original crew at Baer Field, Ft Wayne, Indiana, in December 1942. They are, back row (left to right), Sgt Joe Dicke (flight engineer/waist gunner), 1Lt Don Towns (pilot) and 2Lt Tim Bullard (co-pilot), and in the front row, Sgt Jack Meadows (bombardier) and TSgt Pat DeSantis (turret gunner/radio operator) (*via Franz Reisdorf*)

Zeller and Beard's co-pilot, 1Lt John S Van Epps, later escaped from their Italian PoW camp and returned to the unit on 22 October 1943.

On 28 June, the 320th BG lost B-26B-4 41-18034 *Shootin' Arn* (flown by 1Lt Edwin J Soniat) of the 441st BS on a mission to Milis when flak hit the bomber over the target area. Five parachutes were seen.

BASE MOVE

By late June all three groups again needed to move closer to their targets, with the 17th and 319th BGs transferring to Djedeida, west of Tunis, and the 320th BG heading to Massicault, southwest of the Tunisian capital. Djedeida was the most modern of the North African bases in that it had a hard-surfaced runway. Massicault was yet another dirt strip, however, and was hot in the summer and almost unusable in the winter.

The 319th flew its first mission from its new base on 30 June when it sent bombers to attack Milo airfield. 437th BS B-26C-10 41-34869 was damaged by flak over the target area, and its crew, led by pilot 1Lt Al Graves, ditched the Marauder in the sea. All survived bar the pilot.

The 17th BG sortied from Djedeida for the first time on 3 July when it attacked Milis airfield, on Sardinia – the 320th BG also commenced operations from Massicault that same day, sending B-26s to attack Capoterra, again on Sardinia. Finally, the 17th BG sent 31 B-26s to attack Gerbini airfield, on Sicily, on the 3rd too. Barrage-type flak and 50 Axis fighters were encountered over the target, and 95th BS B-26B-2 41-17924 *Gremlin's Roost*, flown by 1Lt Frank N Dorsey, was shot down.

Two more Marauders were lost the following day when the 319th BG revisited the same target. Axis fighters first claimed 440th BS B-26C-10 41-34872, flown by Capt Griffith P Williams. One of the crew aboard the bomber was group CO Lt Col Wilbur W Aring, flying his 13th mission – he and the rest of the crew baled out into captivity. Coming off the target, the already damaged 440th BS B-26B-15 41-31589, flown by 2Lt Robert Praun, was also downed by fighters. Although only two parachutes were seen, the entire crew escaped the doomed aeroplane except for the pilot, who had been killed during the attack by the fighters.

SSgt Lou Sykes was the turret gunner on board 1Lt Jack Logan's B-26 that day, and he recalled;

'On 4 July 1943 (my eighth mission), we were briefed that our target was the airfield at Gerbini. We were told that we could expect a lot of enemy flak, and that there was an abundance of Axis fighters that would be waiting for us when we got to the target area. Our fighter coverage for this mission was to be the P-38, and due to it having a twin-boom fuselage, it could not possibly be mistaken for any enemy aeroplane.

'As we neared the target, and the flak started darkening the sky, a number of enemy fighters attracted our P-38s away, leaving us unprotected. Once they were some distance away, the flak stopped and we were attacked by another group of fighters.

'I was the top turret gunner, and a fighter came in from high on my left side. I picked him up in my gunsight and gave him several short bursts – my two 0.50-cal guns stopped firing automatically so as not to put any shells through the tail section. The fighter started to smoke, so I got on the intercom to relate this information to the tail gunner, who picked him up and finished off the job that I had started. He got credit for the "kill".

'Another enemy fighter then came in with his guns blazing and tried to break up our six-aeroplane formation by passing as close to the group as possible – some aircraft actually flew through other formations that day as the B-26s took evasive action. We had been briefed to expect this type of attack as the Axis fighters attempted to disrupt our mission.

'The flak then picked up again as we got on our bomb run, and it was extremely accurate. Two of our six aeroplanes had to drop out of formation because of damage, and our four remaining bombers went into a diamond-shaped formation – we were in the rear slot in this group. Once the bombs were released, we started taking evasive action that helped us keep away from where the flak was appearing.

'I knew that our aeroplane had received quite a number of hits, and when we got back to base, it was my duty to examine the top portion of the B-26 to check for damage. I found many small holes, all of which were about the size of a silver dollar. However, there was one hole approximately three feet forward of my Plexiglas dome that a baseball could have fitted through! We couldn't see any holes in the belly of the aeroplane to match up to this one, so we assumed that while the bomb-bay doors were open, the shell must have passed through it! We were all happy to get our feet on the ground after this experience.'

On 8 July the 320th BG bombed Gerbini again, and although it suffered no losses over the target, B-26B 41-17792 *Nana*, flown by 1Lt Burns, was destroyed when it crashed on take-off – the crew survived. The following day the 320th bombed the German HQ at Palazzolo, on Sicily.

Shortly after midnight on the 9th, the first Allied parachutists were dropped on Sicily to signal the start of the invasion. Later that same day the 320th BG attempted to bomb Vizzini, and its important railway junction, but missed both, whilst the 17th BG enjoyed more success targeting a road junction at Caltagirone. 320th BG B-26B-10 41-18195 *Feather Merchant* of the 443rd BS was badly damaged by flak over the target and its pilot, Capt Wilbur R 'Mickey' Welch, died when the bomber hit a house while attempting to land on the island of Pantelleria.

Both the 319th and 320th BGs attacked Gerbini again on 11 July, with the former losing 440th BS B-26B-10 41-18273, flown by Lt Thomas G Masters, when it exploded in mid-air after being attacked by a Bf 109. The 17th BG revisited Milo airfield that same day, and this time the 34th BS suffered heavy casualties – 17 aircrew wounded (three of whom later died) and two aeroplanes salvaged due to battle damage.

Amongst the aircraft to be hit by flak was B-26B-2 41-17858 *COUGHIN' COFFIN*, on its 50th mission. It was the second Marauder in the group to reach the 'half-century' mark, the first one having been 37th BS B-26B-2 *HELL CAT. COUGHIN' COFFIN* was being flown by 1Lt Fred Meher on 11 July, with its original pilot, Maj Pritchard, having come along for its 50th mission as an observer. Despite the aircraft's left engine and hydraulic system being knocked out by flak over the target, the B-26 managed to limp home on the power of just one R-2800.

The crew could only extend the bomber's nose and left main undercarriage legs as it neared Djedeida, and *COUGHIN' COFFIN* tore off the outer section of its right wing as it ground to a halt upon landing. The crew emerged from the bomber unscathed. The veteran B-26 was subsequently repaired and sent home to help sell war bonds.

The 320th BG attacked the Canicatti railway marshalling yards on 12 July, followed by the landing grounds at Carcitella the next day. On the 14th, the group targeted a road junction northeast of Enna, whilst the 319th bombed the heavily defended port of Messina. 439th BS B-26B-10 41-18296, flown by 1Lt Robert W Ruttencutter, was hit by flak over the target area and forced to ditch off the Sicilian coast.

B-26B-2 41-17903 *HELL CAT* was in service with the 37th BS/17th BG from 18 November 1942, and it may have also flown with the 319th BG for a time too. Indeed, 1Lt Ashley Woolridge of the the latter group is seen here posing in the pilot's seat. Woolridge flew 88 missions with the 319th BG before he took command of the 320th BG on 3 November 1944. *HELL CAT's* original pilot was Capt David B Taggart. 41-17903 was the first of the 17th BG's Marauders to complete 50 missions, and it too returned to the US for promotional duties on 15 July 1943 (*Author*)

TARGETING THE ITALIAN MAINLAND

Allied fighter units had started occupying captured airfields on Sicily in mid-July, and by operating from these bases they now had the range to escort Twelfth Air Force bombers tasked with targeting Axis airfields and transportation systems on the Italian mainland that were being used to support enemy forces holding out on the island.

On 16 July the 17th and 319th BGs bombed Vibo Valentia airfield, and 24 hours later they were joined by the 320th BG (flying its 50th mission) in an all out effort against the central railway marshalling yard in Naples. A force of 100+ Marauders hit the target with 500-lb bombs, despite being opposed by heavy flak. A number of aircraft were shot down, including 34th BS B-26Bs 41-17826 *Speed Widget*, flown by 2Lt Helterbrand, and 41-17757 *Ole 757*, flown by Flt Off Warren Faux. The 17th BG also lost B-26B-10 41-18193 *Junior*, flown by 95th BS CO Maj Charles H Diamond and his co-pilot group CO Lt Col Charles R Greening. The bomber crashed near Mt Vesuvius after the crew had baled out.

The 319th BG lost B-26B-10 41-18248, flown by Lt John B Turner of the 438th BS, whilst the 320th had two Marauders shot down. 1Lt Morris M Thompson of the 442nd BS ditched B-26B-3 41-17964 in the sea off Naples, and its crew clambered into rafts and was later rescued. B-26B-4 41-18002, flown by 1Lt Lewis H Braden of the 441st BS, suffered a direct flak hit and disintegrated – there were no survivors. 441st BS B-26B-2 41-17855 *Lady Eve*, flown by Capt Curtiss A Miller, limped away from the target area on one engine and eventually landed in a wheat field near Bizerte, in Tunisia. This epic flight had set a new distance record for a singled-engined Marauder of 350 miles. *Lady Eve* was, however, damaged beyond repair and never flew again.

The 319th and 320th BGs attacked Rome for the first time on 19 July. Although the Germans had not yet occupied the 'Eternal City', it was a staging point for most rail traffic coming down through Italy. As such, it contained many worthwhile military targets.

In May Pope Pius XII had written to President Franklin D Roosevelt requesting that Rome be spared from bombing, and possible irreparable harm. Roosevelt's response in part was, 'In the event it should be found necessary for Allied aeroplanes to operate over Rome, our aviators are thoroughly informed as to the location of the Vatican, and have been specifically instructed to prevent bombs from falling within Vatican City'. Doolittle was told to avoid hitting the Vatican and other historically significant buildings at all cost.

The main attacks on Rome were made by USAAF B-17s, resulting in hundreds of civilian casualties, but only one site of religious importance was damaged – the Basilica di San Lorenzo fuori le Mura.

The 319th and 320th BGs were tasked with keeping Axis fighters on the ground by hitting Ciampino airfield north, which was situated on the southeast side of the city. Although the expected fighter opposition did not materialise, the 441st BS/320th BG still lost B-26C-25 41-35200, piloted by 1Lt Robert T Patterson. The bomber crashed into the sea during the return flight to Massicault, having apparently been hit by flak over the target area.

Over coming days the Marauder groups pounded the Italian roads, rail system and air defences in preparation for the Allied invasion. On 20 July both the 319th and 320th BGs bombed Vibo Valentia airfield. The latter group then hit the Salerno railway marshalling yards on the 22nd and the 319th bombed Aquino airfield on the 23rd.

The 320th BG attempted to knock out the Marina di Paola railway marshalling yards on 24 July, but the first wave of B-26s missed the target with their 500-lb bombs. A second wave of Marauders from the 443rd BS did succeed in hitting the target, but it was then jumped by an estimated 20-25 fighters. Two of the bombers were flying out of formation at the time of the attack and both were shot down. The aircraft lost were B-26C-5 41-34800, flown by 2Lt Walter R White, and B-26B 41-17763, flown by Flt Off Roscoe D Orr. White's aeroplane hit the sea with both engines alight and exploded, while the other B-26 made a good water landing. Marauder crews in the area immediately notified air-sea rescue at Palermo in the hope that survivors might be found.

On 26 July the group returned to the same target in an effort to render it unusable. Led by Capt Charles Belcher in B-26C-25 41-35176 *Millie*, the 320th claimed numerous direct hits without suffering any losses.

The invasion of Sicily had precipitated the fall of the dictator Benito Mussolini, and on 24 July Italian King Victor Emmanuel III had him arrested. He instructed the Army Chief of Staff, Marshal Pietre Badoglio, to take Mussolini's place. Badoglio immediately started negotiations that were aimed at taking Italy out of the war. Allied optimism would, however, be thwarted by Italian politics and German resistance.

Faced with stubborn German opposition in France and the Low Countries, Prime Minister Winston Churchill had long pushed for an Allied invasion of Italy, which he viewed as being the 'soft underbelly' of occupied Europe. Despite American objections, Churchill got his way, delaying the invasion of northern France for a year. Contrary to the British prime minister's views, German and fascist Italian forces in Italy would fight on until VE-Day. And USAAF B-26s would continue to bomb Italian targets for the next 16 months.

B-26C-15 41-34918 *VENGEANCE* **of the 95th BS/17th BG wore one of the most accomplished nose arts applied to a Marauder bomber during World War 2. The aircraft was assigned to 1Lt Virgil V Cornelison, who was one of the group's original pilots – he and his crew had ferried 95th BS B-26B-2 41-17923 to the MTO in December 1942. Despite its elaborate nose art** *VENGEANCE* **later became** *Chief of The Mediums***, and flew at least 90 missions. Of note is the serial data block that specifies the plane as a B-26-C-16-MO! Such sub-divisions within a production block would usually refer to an in-service modification that had been made – in this instance to a B-26-C-15-MO (***Bruce Kwiatkowski***)**

The 17th BG reached a milestone on 27 July 1943 when it bombed Scalea airfield, and thereby conducted its 100th combat mission. On the 29th the 319th BG visited Aquino airfield, with B-26s dropping 500-lb bombs from a mere 6000 ft – the lowest altitude at which ordnance had been expended since the group's return to combat operations. A single Marauder and its pilot were lost on the mission, 1Lt Ralph DeBaby of the 438th BS (flying B-26B-10 41-18258) being killed when the bomber ditched in the Mediterranean – the rest of his crew were rescued.

In late July the 320th BG unexpectedly moved to El Batan, which had previously been home to the 1st FG. The group flew its first mission from the base, which was only a short distance from Massicault, on 31 July when both it and the 319th BG hit a road junction at Adrano, on Sicily.

The first missions for the 17th and 319th BGs in August occurred on the 4th when they attempted to destroy the railway bridge at Maina di Catanzano, in Italy. Both groups missed their target, although they did inflict some damage on adjacent railway marshalling yards. The 320th BG carried out the 2686th Provisional Wing's last bombing mission to Sicily on 6 August when it hit a road junction at Badiazza. The primary aim of this attack was to interfere with the large-scale military evacuation then being conducted by Axis forces, which were attempting to flee to the Italian mainland. Eleven days later, the last rearguard units surrendered after the Allies captured Messina. Sicily had taken just 38 days to conquer.

Despite almost constant air attacks, the Germans had managed to evacuate more than 40,000 troops, 10,000 vehicles (including 44 tanks) and thousands of tons of ammunition. With Sicily neutralised, the Twelfth Air Force could now concentrate on targets on the Italian mainland. This in turn meant longer missions, and the 2686th Provisional Wing extended the range of its Marauders by installing extra fuel tanks in the rarely used aft bomb-bays, which were then sealed shut.

In an effort to offset the extra weight of the fuel tanks, groundcrews removed two (and in some instances all four) package guns from the forward fuselage of the aircraft. These guns had previously been used for ground strafing (something Twelfth Air Force Marauders rarely did) or for defensive fire against head on attacks made by Axis fighters.

Now focusing its attention squarely on Italy, the Twelfth Air Force was ordered to knock out as many bridges as it could in the lead up to the Allied landings. Due to the many mountains, steep hills and rivers that dominated areas of the Italian mainland, the transport system relied heavily on both road and railway bridges.

In the decades prior to the advent of laser- and GPS-guided weapons, bridges were notoriously difficult to hit. Often, they would require multiple bombing runs and additional missions to ensure their destruction. Visiting the same target more than once was always dangerous, as the defences were prepared for another attack. In the Allies' favour was the fact that many bridges were in remote areas. This meant that they were difficult to defend and repair – indeed, some bridges that were hit remain derelict to this day. Many bombardiers devised their own tactics for hitting these targets, and they would get plenty of opportunity to put them to use, as most bridges were repeatedly attacked.

Following its unsuccessful first strike on 4 August, the 17th BG returned to the Maina di Catanzano railway bridge on the 7th, only to miss it for a second time. That same day the 319th and 320th BGs attacked bridges spanning the Angitola River, near Pizzo.

The 320th BG's lead bombardier, TSgt Marvin E Fargo, aboard 442nd BS B-26B-10 41-18186 *Feel Free* (flown by Capt Herman L Meyer), could not hit the bridge from the assigned attack angle, so he went around again. As a result, the group dropped an excellent pattern of bombs on and near the northeast end of the target bridge, severing the railway line. Another flight scored hits on the road bridge upstream from the railway bridge, as well as on the road to the southwest of it. Fargo was awarded the DFC for his exploits on this mission, but both bridges remained standing.

The 319th and 320th BGs went back the next day and attacked the bridges once again, despite [8]/10ths cloud cover. During the 320th's attack, only two-and-a-half flights dropped on their first pass (and all missed the target), so the formation went round again and hit the northern end of the railway bridge. The 319th BG missed the target entirely, so it returned yet again the next day, only to miss once more. The group bombed the Maina di Catanzano railway bridge instead on 11 August, and crews fared much better as they scored hits at both ends.

On the 12th, the 17th and 320th BGs dropped fragmentation bombs on the Grazzanise landing grounds. Fighters tried to intercept them, but the P-38 escorts ensured that no B-26s were lost. The next day all three groups returned to Rome, and this time they hit the railway marshalling yards. Once again there were no losses, and accurate bombing ensured that only minimal damage was inflicted on other parts of the city.

15 August saw the 320th BG target the Sapri marshalling yards, with 28 B-26s dropping 142 500-lb bombs that destroyed hundreds of rail trucks and started huge fires. Smoke from the latter rose to 5000 ft, and could be seen for ten miles. On 16 August the 319th BG bombed a temporary road bridge spanning the River Angitola that had been erected due to damage caused by previous raids. The 320th hit the Battipaglia railway junction and marshalling yards on the 17th, and the next day the 319th BG attempted to block the entrance to the road tunnel at Punta di Stalletti, but only scored hits on the road itself. On 19 August both the 319th and 320th BGs again hit the Sapri railway marshalling yards.

The 320th BG bombed the Caserta railway junction on 20 August, and lost two Marauders in the process. Capt Curtiss A Miller survived his second crash in little more than a month, this time in B-26C-20 41-35167 *Vic*, when the bomber crashed on take-off, whilst the aircraft flown by 1Lt Owen was damaged by fighters over the target and crash-landed on Sicily. Both aeroplanes were destroyed.

The 319th and 320th BGs bombed the Villa Literno railway marshalling yards on the 21st, and were intercepted by an estimated 75 fighters as they approached the target. The 320th bore the brunt of the attacks until escorting P-38s intervened, but not before the enemy had downed four 441st BS

B-26B-2 41-17882 *'The RENAISSANCE'* of the 37th BS/17th BG was the Marauder with the highest number of missions to its credit by the end September 1943. It was returned to the US for promotional duties in November, by which time it had completed 75 missions. This aircraft, stripped of paint, but still with its nose art intact, would later be offered for sale by a salvage company in California for the 'bargain' price of $8500 (*Don Enlow*)

Marauders. The aircraft lost were B-26B-4 41-18001, flown by 1Lt Curtis S Church, B-26B-2 41-17946, flown by 1Lt James W Vandegrift, B-26C-20 41-35145, flown by 1Lt Harold W Dobney and B-26B-4 41-18060, flown by 1Lt Ambrose J Riley. Dobney would later return to the unit at the end of November, having escaped from a hospital in Italy. He travelled 50 miles over mountains with other escaped PoWs, fighting with partisans and hiding from the Germans until he eventually reached Allied lines.

The Axis fighters did not have it all their own way though, with gunners from the 320th BG claiming no fewer than 26 Bf 109s destroyed and a further 14 probably destroyed!

Flight leader Capt Lawrence E Horras of the 441st BS and Mission Commander Capt Jack A Sims (who was also CO of the 444th BS) were both awarded DFCs for the roles they played in this difficult operation.

On 22 August both groups went to the Salerno railway marshalling yards, and this time it was the 319th that sustained the most losses during running battles with an estimated 60 Bf 109s. Coming off the target, no fewer than five 319th BG Marauders were lost, namely B-26C-20 41-35038, flown by 1Lt Dale D Garber of the 439th BS, B-26B-10 41-18217, flown by 1Lt William D Parrish of the 437th BS, B-26C-20 41-35064, flown by 2Lt Alfred R McKenzie of the 438th BS, B-26C-15 41-34936, flown by 1Lt William C Brown of the 438th BS, and B-26B-10 41-18256 *Big Fat Mama*, flown by 1Lt Bradford of the 440th BS – the latter ditched and the crew was rescued.

Maj Joseph Scott Peddie of the 443rd BS, who had led the 320th BG as Mission Commander aboard B-26B-15 41-31601 *Mean Young'Un*, was awarded the DFC for the mission.

The Marauder men were unimpressed with the escort provided on the 22nd by North American A-36s (the ground attack version of the P-51) of the Sicily-based 64th FG – this was the first time that the group had worked with the B-26s. The crews felt that the A-36 boasted insufficient performance at 15,000 ft to allow the fighter to provide the level of close support that they needed when at their bombing altitude. And despite warnings about the similarity of the type to the Bf 109, several B-26 gunners fired on the A-36s nonetheless, which may have been the reason why they kept their distance during this disastrous mission.

On 26 August all three groups raided the Grazzanise landing grounds near Naples, and this time they were challenged by 30-40 fighters. 319th BG B-26C-15 41-34930, flown by 1Lt Gwynn H Robinson of the 439th BS, developed engine problems coming off the target. After dropping behind the main formation, the bomber was attacked by 12 Bf 109s, but the gunners put up a spirited defence and claimed five of the attackers destroyed. The heavily damaged Marauder eventually ditched in the Mediterranean, and its crew was quickly rescued and returned to the unit.

Railway marshalling yards were targeted by Marauder groups during the last week of August, with the 17th and 319th BGs bombing Caserta on the 27th, all three groups attacking the Aversa yards on the 28th, and the 17th and 320th BGs hit Torre Annunziata on the 29th.

At the end of August the 2686th Provisional Wing was redesignated the 42nd Bombardment Wing (Medium).

INVASION OF ITALY

At 0430 hrs on 3 September 1943, the Allies launched Operation *Baytown*, which saw British and Canadian troops of the Eighth Army land on the Italian mainland at Calabria after crossing from Sicily via the Strait of Messina. It was hoped that this operation would draw the enemy away from the main invading force that was soon to go ashore at Salerno, south of Naples, as part of Operation *Avalanche*.

To help further reduce Axis defences in preparation for the invasion, all three B-26 groups of the 42nd BW again attacked the Grazzanise landing grounds on 5 and 6 September, destroying yet more enemy aircraft found at the various airfields in this area.

On the 7th and 8th the groups went after the railway bridge south of Sapri, which they had failed to knock out in previous missions sent to bomb the nearby railway marshalling yards. This time they finally scored hits on this elusive target. The 442nd BS/320th BG lost a Marauder to flak over the target area on the 7th, the crew of B-26B-4 41-18048, flown by 1Lt Morris M Thompson, salvoing their bombs and taking to their parachutes before the aeroplane spun in.

The Allies had secretly signed an armistice with Italy on 3 September, and five days later, following pressure by the Allies, Marshal Pietre Badoglio announced the formal surrender and then formed a government-in-exile in Bari, on the Adriatic Sea coast. The following month he declared war on the Axis powers that still controlled the industrial north of the country. Despite the surrender of Italian forces in the south, 20 months of fighting still lay ahead for the Allies as they engaged 'co-belligerent' Axis troops in central and northern Italy.

On 9 September the 17th and 319th BGs attacked Scanzano landing ground near Taranto in support of Operation *Slapstick* – the British landing to capture this important Italian naval base. The US Fifth Army came ashore at Salerno that same day, and all three groups helped Allied forces establish themselves in Italy by bombing road junctions at Formia, Insernia, Migano and Torre Annunziata over the next few days.

At briefings on 14 September aircrew were told of the desperate situation facing the Salerno beachhead. Field Marshal Albrecht Kesselring, who commanded German forces in Italy, had not been fooled by the British landings to the south and had deployed General Oberst Heinrich-Gottfried von Vietinghoff's 10th Army ready to attack the main invasion force. Wehrmacht troops in the immediate area of the Allied beachhead were supported by one SS and two regular army Panzer divisions, and they would almost succeed in thwarting the invasion.

Outgunned, the US Army requested that the Twelfth Air Force target German forces that were threatening to overwhelm the beachhead.

Round the clock missions were duly flown for 48 hours on 14-15 September, with some crews completing four sorties during this period.

On the 14th, during a 320th BG mission to bomb a road junction at Auletta, B-26C-20 41-35025, flown by Maj Jack A Sims of the 442nd BS, was damaged by flak and diverted to Sicily. Both Sims and his bombardier, Capt James H Macia, were 'Doolittle Raiders', and they became the first B-26 aircrew in the MTO to fly 40 missions and complete a combat tour. That same day, 441st BS B-26B-20 41-18191 *So What*, flown by 1Lt Lawrence J Hayward, crashed when taking off on its second sortie for 14 September.

The Auletta operation was the first mission to be flown by 42nd BW B-26s marked up with new 'battle numbers' (B/N) applied in white on their tails, as per a directive issued by the Twelfth Air Force.

By now the German counterattack against Salerno had stalled, and as enemy forces began to withdraw on 16 September, the 320th BG targeted them as they passed through Formia.

The invasion of southern Italy had made the Axis defence of Sardinia and Corsica untenable, and German and Italian troops had evacuated the islands by month-end. Former enemy airfields on both islands would subsequently be occupied by Twelfth Air Force Marauder units.

All three groups bombed the landing ground at Pratica di Mare on 17 September, the 319th and 320th BGs returning to this target the next day too. The raids saw airfield facilities, and many of the 200+ German and Italian aircraft caught on the ground there, destroyed. B-26C-20 41-35147 B/N 83, flown by Capt William R Barrett, was damaged by flak over the target and a member of its crew killed. The aeroplane was subsequently destroyed crash-landing upon its return from this mission.

Proof that these anti-airfield strikes were having an effect on the Luftwaffe came during the attacks on Pratica di Mare, when the Marauder units went about their business unopposed on both dates, despite having no escorts. And B-26 units would fly repeatedly over enemy territory in coming weeks without the protection of Allied fighters, devastating the rail and road infrastructure used by German forces retreating from the Salerno area.

The 17th BG bombed the Formia railway marshalling yards on 20 September, and the 320th BG made the Twelfth Air Force's first (failed) attempt to hit the Cancello ed Arnone road and railway bridges on the 21st. The 444th BS lost B-26B-2 41-17861 B/N 87 *Dangerous Dan*, flown by 1Lt Daniel Hallowell, on the latter mission. Most of the crew baled out, leaving the pilots to crash-land the bomber – all returned safely.

On 22 September the 319th BG bombed a bridge south of Amorosi, whilst the 17th BG again attacked the road junction at Migano.

The 319th opened the Twelfth Air Force's campaign against yet another difficult target the following day when it attacked the road and railway bridges northeast of Capua. Once again the targets were missed, and the only positive note to come from the operation was the fact 1Lt Robert J Paulsen became the first man in the group to reach his required 40 missions to complete his combat tour and return home.

That same day, the 320th BG went back to the Cancello ed Arnone road and railway bridges, and this time scored at least four direct hits. However, the 319th BG's attempts to bomb a road junction at Avelino the next day met with abject failure. To make matters worse, the group lost B-26C-20 41-35138, flown by 1Lt Callat of the 440th BS, after it dropped out of formation and crash-landed at Termoli.

On the 24th, the 17th BG also hit the road junction at Migano, whilst the 320th BG's 443rd and 444th BSs failed in their attempt to bomb the bridges at Cancello ed Arnone once again. The 441st and 442nd BSs enjoyed more success, however, scoring probable hits on the southern end of a bridge south of Amorosi. Both the 319th and 320th BGs returned to the railway bridge at Cancello ed Arnone on the 25th, and again missed the target. The 320th BG's B-26C-20 41-35030 B/N 06 *Miss Georgie*, flown by 1Lt Carl E Hoy of the 441st BS, was damaged by flak over the target area and was salvaged following a crash-landing on its return to base. That same day the 17th BG tried its luck against the Capua road and railway bridges, but without any success.

Rain led to the cancellation of most missions at the end of September, with bases in North Africa being waterlogged or targets in Italy obscured by low cloud. Conditions at Massicault became so bad that the 320th BG operated many of its B-26s from the 17th and 319th BG base at Djedeida.

On 29 September the 319th BG managed to attack the railway bridge at Cancello ed Arnone, and finally scored hits on its northern end. 439th BS B-26B-10 41-18316 *Charlotte the Harlot*, piloted by 1Lt Basil B Burnstad (who was flying his 40th mission), was shot down by flak over the target. Known as 'Bumstead', to his friends, Burnstad and three gunners hid and waited for Allied troops to advance. His co-pilot and bombardier, who baled out further behind enemy lines, were hidden by a priest until they too were returned to the unit.

The 319th BG redoubled its efforts against the Capua road and railway bridge on 30 September, with the first of that day's two missions being the group's 100th of the war. Unfortunately, the B-26s missed the target on both occasions. The group was thwarted by cloud on 1 October, and missed the target for a third time on its first mission on the 3rd. A second wave from the 319th finally hit the Capua bridge 30 minutes later.

On 4 October the 319th BG attacked a railway overpass at Mignano, scoring many hits, whilst the 320th BG targeted road defiles at Terracina. On the 5th, the 320th bombed a junction near Isernia, whilst the 319th BG gained partial hits on the northern end of a 'horseshoe' road defile at Mignano – the same target was missed the next day by the 320th BG.

On their return from Italy on 5 October, bad weather forced many Marauders to divert, and some crash-landed. 443rd BS B-26B-10 41-18294 B/N 57, flown by 1Lt Robert W Swigart, ground looped at Sidi Ahmed, and 443rd BS B-26B-4 41-17987 B/N 25, flown by 2Lt Edward G Davis, crashed at the same location. Elsewhere, B-26C-20 41-35025 B/N 95, flown by 1Lt John C Edwards of the 444th BS, crashed at Sedjenina.

The 319th BG bombed a road junction at Insernia on 6 October, and that same day the 17th BG was temporarily removed from combat. The group's bombing results had declined so drastically that a period of intensive training was required in order to restore its combat effectiveness. Command changes were also made at group and squadron level, with personnel being brought in from other units to replace officers who had failed to provide the 17th with effective leadership.

B-26B-40 42-43291 B/N 61 *Eightball* of the 95th BS/17th BG drops its bombs on an Italian target defended by a heavy concentration of flak. The three B-26 groups in the MTO lost more Marauders to flak than any other cause – 134 downed by flak, 71 by fighters and 85 to other combat-related causes. In return, the B-26 gunners claimed 304 enemy aircraft destroyed in the air. Photographed here between October and December 1943, as evidenced by its white battle number, *Eightball* flew 167 missions and survived the war. The bomber also retains the red surround to its national insignia (*Louise Hertenstein*)

The weather brought a halt to missions flown by the other two groups for the next week, operations resuming once again on 13 October when B-26s hit the town of Alife with 1000-lb bombs.

The Twelfth Air Force switched from tactical to strategic targets at this time, with both Marauder groups attempting to bomb the railway bridge south of Orvieto on the 14th. The 319th BG could not drop its bombs due to solid cloud cover, whilst the 320th turned back before reaching the target because of fuel concerns. This was the longest mission flown by either group in World War 2, with Orvieto being some 900 miles from El Bathan. Indeed, aircraft were forced to refuel at Sardinia on the mission's return leg.

On 20 October the 319th BG bombed the Montalto di Castro railway bridge and scored possible hits, whilst the 320th BG successfully attacked the railway bridge west of Guardea. 441st BS B-26C-15 41-34912 *Ramblin Reck*, flown by 1Lt John J Turner, left the formation with a smoking engine prior to reaching the target and crashed into the sea. Turner and co-pilot 2Lt John R Smart were both killed and the rest of the crew captured.

The following day the 319th BG attempted to bomb the railway bridge at Marsciano, but actually hit a road bridge north of Acquapendente instead. That same day the 320th BG went after a railway bridge north of Todi, but finding the target obscured by cloud, the Marauders successfully attacked the Montalto di Castro railway bridge instead.

Both groups returned to the railway bridge south of Orvieto on the 22nd, and although the 319th BG missed the target, the 320th put bombs squarely on it. Shortly after leaving the area, Bf 109s made a rare appearance and attacked the 320th BG formation. The fighters succeeded in damaging seven Marauders, and the turret gunner SSgt Dennis O Brown in B-26B-10 41-18189 B/N 15 *Dusty's Devil* (flown by 1Lt Carl E Hoy) was killed when he was hit by a 20 mm cannon shell.

On the 23rd the 319th BG attempted to hit the Marsciano railway bridge again, and this time scored possible hits. The 320th BG was unable to reach its primary target – a railway bridge north of Todi – because its aircraft had used up too much fuel during a difficult form-up with the 319th BG at the start of the mission, so the group attacked the Marsciano railway bridge as well. Again Axis fighters attempted to disrupt the 320th BG, but its gunners, and escorting 1st FG P-38s, prevented any losses.

The following day, the 319th BG attempted to bomb the Terni railway viaduct, but its crews found the target hard to locate and scored no hits.

The 319th BG was attacked by enemy fighters for the first time in a month during this mission, but again there were no losses. The 320th BG returned to Orvieto on the 24th, and this time its target was a railway bridge to the southeast of the city. Finding the bridge obscured by cloud cover, crews bombed their alternate target instead – a railway bridge to the northeast of the city. Most bombs fell wide of the target, which was obscured by smoke from previous attacks by B-25s.

Combat operations were halted for the next few days to allow the ground echelons to move to Sardinia.

The 320th BG ended the month when 35 of its B-26s dropped 234 500-lb demolition bombs on Anzio harbour on the 31st. The target was well covered, and there were no losses. On 1 November the 320th BG joined the 319th BG at Djedeida, prior to moving to Sardinia.

The 320th attempted to bomb the railway bridge at Marsciano that same day, but fog prevented them attacking either the primary or secondary targets. The crews therefore bombed a target of last resort – the harbour installations at Civitavecchia. 442nd BS B-26B-10 41-18186 B/N 37 *Feel Free* crashed on take-off when pilot 1Lt Charles P Speegle apparently caught his foot on a rudder pedal. The next day, the 319th BG flew its last mission from Djedeida when bombers targeted the Terni railway viaduct. Although hits were scored, the viaduct was left standing.

OPERATIONS FROM SARDINIA

During the first week of November 1943, the 319th and 320th BGs moved to Decimomannu airfield, on Sardinia. Just a few months earlier this had been one of their former targets, and USAAF engineers had to spend a number of weeks repairing bomb damage created by the B-26s prior to it being deemed ready for the 42nd BW! Decimomannu's 2000-yard-long runway was also 500 ft wide, and this allowed the 319th BG CO, Col Joseph R Holzapple, to introduce multi-aircraft take-offs. From now on a flight of three B-26s could take off at the same time with a mere ten feet of separation between them. Such take-offs significantly reduced form-up times, thereby saving fuel and increasing the range of the bombers.

The group's first mission that utilised this procedure occurred on 12 November, when bombers targeted railway lines between Tarquinia and Montalto di Castro. It was deemed to be too dangerous to continue

Decimomannu's 500-ft wide runway allowed the 319th BG CO Col Joseph R Holzapple to introduce three-ship take-offs, as seen here. The first mission to employ this method was the attack on the railway line between Tarquinia and Montalto di Castro mounted on 12 November 1943. The procedure reduced form-up times by 13 minutes, thereby adding an extra 50 miles to the group's combat radius if required. The nearest Marauder is 41-31985 B/N 15 *Charlotte the Harlot II* of the 437th BS. This aeroplane was the replacement for B-26B-10 41-18316 *Charlotte the Harlotte*, which was brought down by flak whilst attacking a railway bridge northeast of Capua on 29 September 1943. B-26B-45 MA 42-95776 B/N 15 was named *Charlotte the Harlot III*, and the bomber crashed on take-off on 17 April 1944. It was duly replaced by B-26G-5 43-34243 B/N 15 *Charlotte the Harlot IV* (*Louise Hertenstein*)

multi-aircraft take-offs during the winter, although they would be re-introduced in the spring of 1944 – by which time the runway had been made even wider to enable the group to conduct six-aircraft take-offs.

Unlike the 319th BG's three-aircraft formations, the 320th BG often introduced a fourth bomber to its flights, so it was limited to this number taking off at once. The B-26's chequered reputation came to the fore again at this time, with multi-aircraft take-offs initially being viewed with some concern by crews due to the increased possibility of accidents. If an aeroplane was to lose power on take-off it could slew sideways into another bomber in the formation. Yet despite these concerns, such an accident never actually happened.

The compacted soil runway did become spongy when wet, however, and this added strain to the B-26's undercarriage, causing a number of additional gear collapses on landing. Yet these problems were more than offset for the crews by the big improvement in their living conditions on Sardinia when compared with the dirt bases that they had had to endure in North Africa.

Despite Sardinia being a constitutive part of Italy, the locals showed little respect for the 'Italian war', and were welcoming to the Americans. The men were particularly impressed by how far their money would go, as everything was much cheaper on the island – haircuts cost five cents, superior wine 50 cents and the company of a woman just 15 cents!

Poor weather continued to hamper operations in November, with many missions being cancelled over coming weeks. On 12 November the 17th BG was at last deemed ready to return to combat following 37 days of solid remedial training, although it had to delay operations from its new base at Villacidro, five miles from Decimomannu, as the airfield was waterlogged. The group was instead forced to operate from Djedeida for a short period of time, launching the first of nine missions flown from the base on 12 November when B-26s attacked the railway line at Orbebello, 50 miles north of Rome.

All three groups were to continue their missions against airfields, bridges or railway marshalling yards over coming weeks, with the Sardinia-based B-26 units now also being able to hit targets in southern France. The 319th and 320th BGs flew the wing's first mission to this country on 16 November when they attacked the airfield at Salon. Ju 88s and He 111s armed with radio-controlled glide bombs were based here, and they had enjoyed some success targeting Allied shipping in the Mediterranean over previous months.

The 319th BG bombed first, and although an estimated ten to fifteen Bf 109s attacked the formation, there were no losses thanks to effective escorting by P-38s from the 14th FG. The USAAF fighters could not prevent the loss of 320th BG Marauder B-26C-20 41-35029 B/N 08, flown by 1Lt Nathanial S Robbins, however, the bomber losing an engine to flak over the target area and crash-landing at Alghero, on Sardinia, without injury to the crew.

Both the 319th and 320th BGs were sent to bomb the railway marshalling yards at Arrezzo on 26 November, although cloud cover prevented the groups from dropping their bombs. The mission proved to be disastrous for the 440th BS/319th BG, which lost three Marauders either in a mid air collision or to severe icing in cloud – they all crashed into the Mediterranean. The bombers lost were B-26C-10 41-34867 B/N 80, flown by 2Lt Frank R Buckner, B-26B-10 41-18215 B/N 86 *Dirty Bird*, flown by 1Lt Harry F Kress, and B-26B-15 41-31591 B/N 73 *The Elmer Fudd*, flown by 1Lt Paul S Worley.

Witnesses in other aeroplanes thought that they saw two bombers going down together, and a third B-26 cartwheeling in. Two oil slicks and debris were seen on the water, but no survivors were found.

Accidents continued to take their toll of Marauders in the other two groups as well. Departing on a mission that targeted the airfield at Salon-de-Provence, in France, on 28 November, B-26B-40 42-43280 B/N 06 *Donna Y*, flown by 1Lt Clarence E Cotty, blew a tyre on take-off and crashed. That same day, the 17th BG's B-26B-10 41-18265 *Ruthless* of the 37th BS had its undercarriage collapse on landing and was destroyed. The latter group also lost the CO of the 432nd BS, Maj Belsma, on a raid against the railway bridge at Monte Molino on 30 November when the lead ship, B-26B-10 41-18187 B/N 81 *The Wolves*, flown by Capt Morris McCarver, was shot down over Vieano, in Italy.

On 7 December Maj Charles G Robinson, acting group CO of the 319th BG, decided to modify his group's tactics by sending out a single Marauder on a low-level attack. He wanted to see if a B-26 attacking from this height could achieve the same level of destruction against a target as a group of bombers dropping ordnance from a higher, safer, but less accurate, altitude. He and a volunteer pilot duly flew two single-aircraft missions against the Var River railway bridge in France. Robinson could not drop his bombs due to cloud cover, but the other B-26, flown by 1Lt George T Stannard, attacked a railway bridge south of Taggia, on Italy's northern border. The results of the attack were not seen before the crews went on to strafe shipping on the return leg of their mission.

On 18 December, the 320th BG attempted to hit the Antheor railway viaduct once again, but missed. The flak was heavy and accurate, damaging 12 of the 39 Marauders sortied. There was also one fatality – SSgt Wesley D Dolan, top turret gunner aboard 442nd BS B-26C-15 41-34999 B/N 33 *'Shif'less'*, flown by 1Lt Richard A Dodelin, was decapitated when an 88 mm shell detonated near his crew station. Engineer/waist gunner SSgt Joseph Garbenches, despite having been wounded by the same shell, extricated Dolan's body and manned the turret for the rest of the mission. He was awarded the DFC for his actions.

That same day the 319th BG bombed two road and railway bridges next to each other spanning the Var River, near Nice. The targets were well hit, and there was no opposition. Reconnaissance photographs later showed that the highway bridge had collapsed and the railway bridge had been hit three times. All three groups bombed railway marshalling yards and/or bridges the following day. The 319th BG's target was the railway bridge and yards at Foligno, and although the latter was hit, the

Two Marauders from the 432nd BS/ 17th BG that had the same name and battle number were B-26B-10 41-18187 B/N 81 *"THE WOLVES"* and B-26B-45 42-95765 *"THE WOLVES"*. The former had flown more than 40 missions by the time it was shot down over Vieano on 30 November 1943 whilst being flown by Capt Morris McCarver. Its replacement, 42-95765, survived the war. The latter is shown early in its combat career prior to the reclining nude being clothed in response to an order issued by the 42nd BW (*Bruce Kwiatkowski*)

B-26C-25 41-35177 B/N 17 *UDEN UDEN'S OIL BURNER* of the 34th BS/17th BG is escorted home with its engine feathered following a mission to the Rocca Secca bridge on 30 December 1943. Its pilot, 1Lt Tilman Beardon, had ordered everything jettisoned to help the bomber retain its altitude on one engine – a 0.50-cal ammunition belt has just been thrown out of the waist window. The aircraft was named for the wife of the pilot's instructor, who had been killed in a training accident. It sports the early white battle number on the fin, which was later changed to red, edged with white. The aeroplane escorting 41-35177 is B-26B-40 42-43272 B/N 87 *Hawkeye* of the 432nd BS, which has had the forward part of its propeller bosses painted white to denote the bomber's squadron assignment. It is interesting to note that both the B-26s in this photograph still sport the short-lived red surround to the national insignia some four months after it was supposed to have been replaced with insignia blue (*Alf Egil Johannessen*)

bridge was missed. Returning from the target, 440th BS B-26C-10 41-34881 B/N 77 *Miss Eveready*, flown by 1Lt Walden R Stewart, was hit by flak over Orvieto and only three parachutes were seen before the aeroplane crashed.

On 23 December, the 320th BG attacked the railway bridges at Ventimiglia, in Italy, and although the group succeeded in hitting the approaches to the west bridge and the nearby tunnel entrance, it missed both bridges. That same day the 319th BG attacked the railway viaduct at Antheor for the first time. The group scored direct hits on the target, but the bombs were deemed to be insufficient in size to destroy the robust viaduct. Lancasters of the RAF's Nos 619 and 617 Sqns (the latter unit famous for its dams raid in May 1943) had failed to destroy the viaduct with 12,000-lb high-capacity bombs three months earlier.

The Marauders encountered heavy flak over the target, and were also attacked by fighters. No losses were suffered, however, and B-26 gunners claimed the destruction of a Bf 109 in return.

The 319th and 320th BGs joined forces to attack the Zoagli viaduct, in Italy, on 27 December, scoring several direct hits on the structure. Confusion subsequently reigned when the B-26s returned to land at Villacidro, as the base tower advised crews to go around repeatedly due to one of the runways being obstructed by a 1000-lb bomb. This hung up weapon had fallen out of the bomb-bay of an early-returning 320th BG aeroplane moments after it had touched down. Ordnance personnel decided that they had insufficient time to disarm the bomb before the circling B-26s ran out of fuel, so 437th BS pilot 1Lt Arthur Cruse and a team of volunteers rolled the weapon off the runway, thereby allowing aircraft from both groups to land safely.

ORGANISATIONAL CHANGES

At year-end, the 42nd BW was transferred back to Twelfth Air Force control, with XII Bomber Command in turn being assigned to the Mediterranean Allied Tactical Air Forces (MATAF). These changes had little impact on the trio of B-26 groups on Sardinia, which continued to attack transport-related targets in Italy and France.

To end the year Capt Lawrence J Hayward of the 320th BG's 441st BS flew with a volunteer crew on an unescorted single aeroplane mission to

attack the railway bridge at Albinia, in Italy. The daring raid met no opposition, but cloud completely obscured the target so the B-26 returned to base with its bombs.

January 1944 saw the continuation of the campaign against the Italian rail network. The bombing accuracy of the Marauders was increasing all the time, but some of the bridges needed repeated attention. Targets were missed, partially destroyed or had to be bombed again following repairs. On 2 January, 26 Marauders of the 320th BG bombed the railway bridges at Ventimiglia, achieving an 86 per cent strike rate and completely destroying the western bridge. Bombs also hit the road bridge just east of the target railway bridges.

That same day the 319th BG returned to attack railway bridges over the Var River, near Nice. The group left one of the bridges unserviceable by destroying repairs that had been carried out since its previous raid.

The 320th BG began the 42nd BW's campaign against the heavily defended 70-ft road bridge at Roccasecca, just behind the German frontline, on 3 January. The group scored hits in the target area, but left with the bridge still standing. Intense flak damaged 19 of the 28 Marauders participating in the mission, including 443rd BS B-26B-10 41-18288 B/N 62 *Scramboogie*, flown by 1Lt Rucker. Lead navigator Capt Joseph R Cafarella guided the aeroplane through the flak, despite being wounded, and gave first aid to seriously wounded bombardier 2Lt Kenneth A Grant. Cafarella was later awarded the DFC for his actions. 2Lt Kenneth Strachan, flying B-26C-15 41-34922 B/N 68 *Fukup*, escorted both *Scramboogie* and another damaged Marauder (B-26C-15 41-34907 B/N 1, flown by 1Lt James T Paulantis) back to an Allied airfield at Pomigliano, near Naples.

Two 18-aircraft formations from the 17th and 319th BGs attempted to hit the bridge the next day, but all returned with their bomb loads intact due to the target being obscured by cloud. The 320th BG tried again on the 7th, and although it scored hits on the western approaches, the bridge was left unscathed.

On 9 January the 319th BG returned to Roccasecca, sending three waves of 12 B-26s over the bridge in just a matter of minutes. The first formation finally destroyed the target, and the group suffered no losses.

The first ever night mission flown by the 42nd BW was carried out on 10 January when the 320th BG CO, Lt Col Eugene B Fletcher, flying B-26C-45 42-107795 B/N 11 *Little Catherine*, led a three-aircraft mission to the Piombino iron and steel works. The aeroplanes took off at 2000 hrs, and reached Piombino less than an hour later. All bombs landed within the target area, with direct hits recorded on the blast furnaces and works buildings. The defences were taken by surprise, and only a few bursts of inaccurate flak were encountered immediately above the target itself – none of the B-26s were damaged. Fletcher was awarded the DFC for the mission.

Another unusual operation was flown two days later when the 17th BG bombed the Isoletta dam on the Liri River. Heavy flak claimed two 34th BS Marauders on this mission, B-26B-15 41-31582 B/N 05, flown by 1Lt Aubrey Cooper, exploding overhead the target, and damaged B-26B-10 41-18253 B/N 02 *Phoebe* being wrecked in a crash-landing upon its return to Villacidro.

This as yet unidentified insignia adorned the nose of B-26B-15 41-31582 B/N 05 of the 34th BS/17th BG. It was one of two Marauders lost by the group during an attack on the Isoletta dam, on the Liri River, on 12 January 1944. 1Lt Aubrey Cooper was flying 41-31582 when it exploded over the target, whilst the damaged B-26B-10 41-18253 B/N 02 *Phoebe* was wrecked in a crash landing upon its return to Villacidro (*Bruce Kwiatkowski*)

B-26B-45 42-95759 B/N 63 *TIGER LADY* of the 443rd BS/320th BG, seen here in lead ship configuration with the astrodome atop the fuselage. Lt Col Eugene Fletcher was observing his group's bombing of the Orte railway marshalling yards from *TIGER LADY's* astrodome on 17 January 1944 when he was hit in the head by flak and had his skull fractured. A lead ship carried a Norden bombsight for use by a lead bombardier. Unusually, 42-95759 retains the lower 0.50-cal machine gun in the nose that was often removed to save space (*via Franz Reisdorf*)

The Twelfth Air Force staged a coordinated attack on Luftwaffe defences around Rome on 13 January, the 17th and 320th BGs bombing Ciampino airfield and the 319th BG targeting the fighter base at Centocelle. Using both parafrags and 500-lb high explosive bombs, the groups destroyed airfield facilities and many aeroplanes that were parked in the open at both locations. Both flak and fighters were encountered, but no B-26s were lost. Following these raids, all remaining Axis aircraft were withdrawn to airfields further north.

Capt Charles P Speegle of the 320th BG's 443rd BS, flying B-26C-20 41-35179 B/N 34 *Oozin Suzan*, was awarded the DFC for leading this successful mission, and the 17th BG was awarded a Distinguished Unit Citation (DUC) for its accurate bombing of Ciampino.

The 319th and 320th BGs revisited the railway bridges at Orvieto on 15 January. When approaching the target, the 320th BG's 443rd BS B-26B-15 41-31575 B/N 60 *Hot Garters*, flown 1Lt Festus D Hunter, was hit by flak. Despite having a wing on fire, Hunter held the aeroplane steady on its bomb run. He was forced to rely on bombardier 1Lt Benjamin E Pickett to guide him to the bridge, as the flak had also knocked out the Pilot Direction Indicator. After leaving the formation, the Marauder was again hit by flak, and Hunter skilfully flew the bomber back to Corsica on just one good engine. Both men received the DFC for their actions.

All three groups flew missions against difficult targets at Orte, 20 miles south of Orvieto, on 16 and 17 January. On the 16th, the 319th and 320th BGs hit railway marshalling yards and a bridge, and the 319th was attacked by fighters whilst on its bomb run. 440th BS B-26C-5 41-34764 B/N 88, flown by 1Lt Owen L Koontz, went down in flames, and 437th BS B-26C-10 41-34887 B/N 16, flown by Flt Off Harold G Kantner, eventually crashed into the Mediterranean after being badly shot up.

The 320th BG also lost two bombers to enemy fighters, B-26C-10 41-34900 B/N 64 *Man-O-War*, flown by 1Lt John R Space, being attacked just prior to commencing its bomb run. Flying in the tail-end position, the aircraft was picked off by fighters and went down near Lake Vico. Minutes later, B-26B-40 42-43315 B/N 87, flown by 1Lt Joseph A Green, and with 444th BS CO Maj James L McCrory also aboard, was hit by flak and set on fire 20 seconds before 'bombs away'. Green continued on course so that bombardier 1Lt James Banicki could drop his bombs. Six or seven parachutes were then seen to emerge from the stricken aeroplane before it exploded. Green survived, and was awarded the DFC.

Three of those killed (including gunner SSgt William A Harrison) were on their 40th mission.

On the 17th, the 17th BG suffered no losses, but again the 320th BG lead ship (B-26B-45 42-95759 B/N 63 *TIGER LADY*, flown by Capt Hunter) was hit by flak. Group CO, Lt Col Fletcher, was hit in the head by shrapnel whilst observing the mission from the astrodome. Suffering a fractured skull that put him in hospital, he would resume his command on 2 March. The B-26 was swiftly replaced in the formation by the group back up aircraft, flown by 1Lt Henry S Saylor, which guided the formation out of the flak.

Saylor's B-26B-45 42-95774 B/N 53 was also hit, and the pilot had to nurse the aeroplane back to Sardinia on one engine. Fletcher was subsequently awarded the Silver Star and Saylor the DFC for their actions during this mission.

The 42nd BW attacked Orvieto again on 21 January, and flak claimed yet more Marauders from both the 319th and 320th BGs. The first aircraft lost was veteran B-26B-10 41-18326 B/N 52 *SKEETER*, flown by 1Lt Clarice A Randall, of the 437th BS/319th BG, which went down in flames over the target. Things then got a lot worse for the 320th BG, as it lost three bombers near Orvieto and a fourth that crash-landed upon its return to base.

Flight leader 1Lt John C Edwards' B-26B-10 42-43276 B/N 78 *Wolfette* was hit during its bomb run, and six parachutes emerged from the flaming aeroplane before it started to spin in – a seventh parachute emerged just before the bomber hit the ground. Edwards was awarded the Silver Star for giving his crew the chance to bale out while he stayed at the controls until the last minute, when he too abandoned the aircraft.

B-26B-2 41-17903 *HELL CAT*'s replacement was B-26 *HELL CAT II*, B-26C-20 41-35159 B/N 35, and it featured almost identical nose art. The latter aircraft was destroyed when it blew a tyre on take-off at Villacidro on 20 January 1944 (*Don Enlow*)

Crew chief TSgt Earl Holtorp poses in front of his charge, B-26B-10 41-18326 B/N 52 *SKEETER* of the 437th BS/319th BG. At the time this photograph was taken, the bomber's mission log indicated that it had flown 56 missions. Holtorp had given the Marauder its name, which was in fact his favourite nickname for his wife. The aeroplane was lost on its 67th mission when, on 21 January 1944, it was hit by flak whilst attacking the bridges at Orvieto (*Don Enlow*)

Right
B-26B-10 41-18305 B/N 14 *Miss Manchester* was one of four 320th BG Marauders lost to flak on the costly mission to Orvieto railway bridge south on 21 January 1944. *Miss Manchester* was replaced by B-26B-50 42-95884 *Miss Manchester* B/N 14, which went on to fly more than 100 missions, and survive the war (*via Franz Reisdorf*)

B-26B-10 41-18305 B/N 14 *Miss Manchester's* nose art featured a female figure sitting on a red bomb. 42-95884 boasted similar artwork, although the bomb was yellow in colour (*via Franz Reisdorf*)

The 441st BS's original *Miss Manchester*, B-26B-4 41-18305 B/N 14, was also hit on the bomb run. Its pilot, 1Lt Robert B Currie, again held the burning aeroplane steady so that his crew could bale out. Five parachutes were seen before the bomber exploded. Currie, who was listed as Missing In Action, was awarded the DFC for his actions.

B-26C-20 41-35070 B/N 04 *Frances Joan* was also seen to leave the formation over the target, and as many as five parachutes were spotted prior to the aircraft crashing near Viterbo.

Finally, B-26B-15 41-31574 B/N 18, flown by Flt Off Elwin C 'Skeets' Goodenough, was badly shot up over the target and crash-landed upon its return to Villacidro.

ANZIO

On 22 January 1944, the Allies made a virtually unopposed landing in the Anzio/Nettuno area of Italy's central west coast, just south of Rome. Code named Operation *Shingle*, it was hoped that the invasion would either draw German forces away from the 'Gustav Line' (the most rearward of the three German defensive lines on the Italian peninsula south of Rome, built along the Garigliano and Rapido rivers), allowing the possibility of a successful Allied assault, or enable a swift advance on Rome.

MATAF medium bombers were tasked with hitting the rail and road network that would be used by German forces heading for the beachhead. All of the 42nd BW's groups flew missions in support of the landings over the next five days, although the weather often thwarted their efforts.

Both the 17th and 319th BGs attempted to destroy the road and railway bridges at Ceprano on 22 January, but they failed to hit the target. The 440th BS/319th BG lost B-26B-45 42-95748, flown by Flt Off Charles LeComte, after it was hit by flak over the target area. The Marauder burst into flames and crashed a short distance from the bridges.

Later that same day, 34 aircraft from the 320th BG dropped an excellent pattern of bombs on a road junction at Velletri. B-26C-25 41-35178 B/N 91, flown by 1Lt Otto Meyer, crashed on take-off for this mission, although the crew escaped unhurt. The next day, the 320th BG failed to bomb the road between Carsoli and Tagliacozzo because of cloud cover, despite making two runs at it. The 319th BG's mission against a road junction at Val Montone was thwarted for the same reason.

On 25 January the 320th BG attempted to bomb the railway marshalling yards at Terni, but cloud cover forced them to attack an identical target at Rieti instead. Poor weather conditions at the latter site ensured that only 17 of the 33 B-26s in the formation dropped their bombs. The group returned to Terni on 27 January.

The wing staged another all out effort against the various bridges at Orvieto on the 28th, with the 17th BG attacking first and stopping a troop train that was in the process of crossing one of the targeted bridges. The 320th BG followed up this initial attack some 15 minutes later, catching many of the fleeing troops in the open. It was credited with destroying the railway bridge.

Once again, the 319th BG's 440th BS was the only unit to suffer

The 439th BS/319th BG crew that named B-26C-11 41-18322 B/N 64 *Hell's Belle II* is shown with the aeroplane after the bomber completed its 51st mission in early 1944. Standing, from left to right, are radio tail gunner Thomas Quigley, bombardier/navigator Charles Schulwolf, co-pilot Waverly Johnson, pilot Jack Logan and engineer/waist gunner Robert Fessenden. In the front row, again from left to right, are two unknown groundcrew, armourer/turret gunner Lou Sykes and crew chief Kenneth Smith (*Lou Sykes*)

losses on this raid. B-26B-10 41-18275 B/N 92 *Little Salvo* lost an engine on take-off and crashed, and B-26B-10 41-18325 B/N 87, flown by flight leader 1Lt Frederick Gedge Jr, was downed by fighters in the target area.

Despite the loss of a bomber to Axis fighters, anti-flak measures employed by the 319th during the course of the mission reduced the amount of damage its B-26s suffered over the target area itself. The four flights from the group attacked from different directions, forcing the defenders to concentrate their fire at just one flight at a time, rather than the whole formation. Two flights from the 319th BG also bombed (and missed) the bridge at Montalto, which was the mission's alternate target.

On 29 January the 320th BG hit the Manziana railway bridge, plastering the target area with 120 1000-lb bombs and scoring some direct hits on the structure. Escorted by Free French Air Force (FFAF) Spitfires, the B-26s encountered both accurate flak and Axis fighters.

Three Marauders were lost to enemy action, one of which was B-26B-45 42-95763 B/N 39 of the 442nd BS, flown by 1Lt Clifford R Conrad. The aeroplane was hit by flak in the bomb-bay prior to commencing its bomb run, but the crew managed to keep it in formation. It was then bounced by fighters, which succeeded in severing the bomber's control cables. The pilot ordered the crew to bale out, but when he learned that several men had been wounded, Conrad wrestled with the controls again and found that he could steer the B-26 by manipulating its trim tabs and using partial rudder – he cancelled the bale out order.

Conrad, turret gunner/engineer SSgt Eugene E Floto and tail gunner SSgt Jerry W Rodgers were awarded DFCs for their bravery in continuing to man their positions despite being wounded – the gunners had defended the damaged B-26 against continued fighter attacks. The crew coaxed the bomber back as far as Corsica, where they all baled out.

B-26B-50 42-95996 B/N 41 *Gunga Din*, flown by 1Lt Elbert O Stephenson, was also hit by flak. Unlike Conrad's Marauder, it caught fire, and flames were spotted escaping from its open bomb-bay by another aircraft in the formation. The pilot managed to close the bomb-bay doors and head south along the coast, enabling the crew to bale out. Seven parachutes were seen before the bomber went down off Ladispoli.

B-26C-15 41-34922 B/N 68 *Fukup*, flown by 2Lt William R Wheeler of the 443rd BS, was attacked by fighters over the target and its tail partly shot away. With one engine afire, the bomber remained in formation for a while and then headed for Corsica with an escort of three B-26s. Radio contact could not be made with the crew, and the aircraft eventually exploded and crashed into the sea 50 miles from Corsica. An oil slick and a flaming Mae West marked the spot where the Marauder hit the water.

On 2 February, squadron commanders within the 42nd BW told their crews that the completion of 40 missions would no longer see them declared tour expired and sent home. From then on, they would fly indefinite tours until they were deemed to be suffering from combat fatigue. 319th BG flight surgeon Dr David O Gorlin, whose job it would be to make judgments on the men's ability to fly combat missions, quipped at the time, 'We have a new 40-mission system. After 40 missions, the flight surgeon automatically becomes a son-of-a-bitch'.

This change came about due to the high number of missions that were flown during the winter of 1943-44. If everyone with 40 missions under

Uffizi gallery and the many churches dotted around the city. Destroying such buildings or irreplaceable works by artists such as Michelangelo and Leonardo Da Vinci would have been a major loss to humanity as well as a public relations disaster for the Allies.

The wing's current record for bombing accuracy augured well, and the yards were duly hit with pinpoint accuracy. The 319th BG was deemed to have performed particularly well, and it was duly awarded its second DUC in eight days for accurate bombing.

On 13 March the 320th BG attempted to hit the Viareggio railway bridge. Although the latter only received some damaging near misses, 40 wagons were destroyed and the line itself cut north of the bridge. That same day the 17th and 319th BGs bombed the Sarzana railway bridge over Magra River with better results. Reconnaissance photographs would later show that three spans had been dropped at one end and a fourth at the other end, thus putting the bridge out of commission. The results achieved by 17th BG was particularly impressive, as all 96 bombs dropped from its 24 Marauders fell within the designated 400-ft target area – the first 100 per cent mission for the 42nd BW, and the 200th operation for the 17th BG.

During the 320th BG's 14 March mission to the Prenestina railway marshalling yards, 443rd BS B-26B-10 41-18328 B/N 59 *Miss Represented*, flown by 2Lt Stinson, had three 500-lb bombs that refused to budge. Despite the possibility of these armed weapons exploding, bombardier Sgt Charles J Szafir disarmed and re-hung them, allowing the bomber to return to base and land safely – Szafir was awarded the DFC for his actions.

The next day all three groups hit the town of Cassino, and Gen Eaker would later state that the B-26s performed the best bombing that he had ever seen during the course of the mission. The 320th BG's 34 B-26s were the last over the target, led by Capt Laurence E Probasco at the controls of 41-31596 B/N 31 *Cornfed Commando*. The lead navigator for the operation, 1Lt Francis J Boyne, and Flight Commander Maj Gordon F Friday were both awarded the DFC for their leadership that day. There was no flak, and the B-26s did not actually overfly enemy territory, as they broke off just after releasing their bombs.

Unfortunately, the concentrated bombing failed to dislodge the German defenders, and the second Allied Cassino offensive had to be called off when troops met fierce resistance in the ruins of the town.

The wing staged another group effort on 16 March when it targeted ground forces in Aquino. The city was one of the strong points in the so-called 'Adolf Hitler Line', which was the fallback position ten miles

B-26C-10 41-18322 B/N 64 *Hell's Belle II* of the 439th BS/319th BG leaves Sarzana railway bridge (bottom of photograph), over the Magra River, on 13 March 1944. Both the 319th and the 17th BGs bombed the target on this date, and reconnaissance photographs would later show that three spans were dropped at one end and another one at the opposite end, thus putting the bridge out of commission. This day was a double landmark for the 17th BG, as all 96 bombs dropped by its 24 Marauders fell within the designated 400 ft target area, thus giving the 42nd BW its first 100 per cent mission. It was also the 17th BG's 200th combat mission of the war (*Louise Hertenstein*)

north of the 'Gustav Line'. The 17th BG lost two 37th BS Marauders and their crews when the bombers (B-26C-20 B/N 32 41-35018 *Spooks*, flown by 1Lt C M Angel, and B-26B-45 42-95782 B/N 26, flown by 2Lt C L Bosch) collided whilst forming up for the mission.

The target was squarely hit, but again flak took its toll. The 320th BG lost B-26B-45 42-95790 B/N 17 *Beauts and Saddles*, flown by 2Lt Francis B Hendrix of the 441st BS, on the breakaway from the target. The aeroplane was hit in the right engine, which in turn started a fire in the nearby wing area. Seven parachutes were seen to emerge from the bomber before the it hit the ground.

OPERATION *STRANGLE*

On 19 March MATAF launched Operation *Strangle*, the aim of which was to weaken German supply lines to their forces defending the 'Gustav Line' in an effort to diminish their ability to defend against an impending Allied offensive. Although the 42nd BW would be attacking the same types of targets it had bombed before (and re-visiting a number it had already attacked), the operation differed from earlier campaigns in that it was conducted by MATAF. And this time the entire Axis railway system of bridges, tunnels, marshalling yards and, in some instances, stretches of track would be bombed.

Sea routes and ports were also hit, all of which was designed to force the Germans to use the inadequate Italian road system. MATAF medium bombers and dedicated ground attack aircraft would then target the enemy's supply system once it started to appear on the roads.

Strangle would last until 10 May, and during this period the wing repeatedly attacked many of the targets it was assigned to bomb such as the bridges at Poggibonsi, Arezzo, Bucine and Incisa. Once again, bridge and viaduct targets would often prove difficult to identify and hit, and on the first day of the operation the 319th BG attempted to knock out the viaduct at Arezzo but actually bombed the wrong target. Other flights in the group dropped on San Stefano with unknown results. The 320th BG managed to hit the Arezzo viaduct, but it remained standing.

The next day, the latter group returned to Orvieto to bomb the northern railway bridge. Only four B-26s dropped on the primary target due to cloud cover, while thirteen others bombed the secondary target of Port Ercole. The bridge was missed, but the town and dock installations in Port Ercole were well hit. Four of the group's B-26s were damaged by flak and fighters, although Marauder gunners claimed two fighters shot down in return. Elsewhere that same day, the 17th BG dropped 2000-lb bombs on Piombino harbour – the first time that bombs of this size had been employed by specially modified B-26s.

All three groups went back to Arezzo on 21 March, and the 17th and 320th BGs put bombs in the area of the viaduct and scored possible hits. The 319th BG's attack on the nearby railway bridge was disrupted by cloud, however, with the lead ship attacking Burine viaduct by mistake. The other flights, spotting the error, dropped on both Cecina and Poggibonsi bridges, which were the alternate targets.

The Poggibonsi railway bridges were revisited the next day by both the 319th and 320th BGs. The lead formation from the 319th missed the target, and the remaining three from the group dropped on the road bridge to the south of the city, rather than the railway bridge to the northwest. Group CO, Col J R Holzapple, blamed the failure of this mission on his bombardiers, who he claimed had not sufficiently studied their maps.

The 320th BG crews fared much better, hitting the road bridge and scoring possible hits on the railway bridge too. Their bombs also cut the tracks with a direct hit. The group did, however, suffer a loss at the start of the mission when B-26B-45 42-95767 B/N 10 *Ozark Queen*, flown by 441st BS CO Capt Elmer G Oglietti, crashed and exploded on take-off. The bomber's co-pilot, 2Lt Oran B Williams, was killed, whilst both Oglietti and the lead bombardier, 1Lt Joseph L Cukar, succumbed to their injuries 48 hours later. The remaining crewmembers were seriously injured, but they recovered.

All three groups attacked the Campo di Marte railway marshalling yards at Florence on 23 March and dropped an excellent pattern of bombs in the assigned area – the 320th BG alone claimed the destruction of an estimated 270 railway trucks. Recently promoted Maj Brewer and lead bombardier 1Lt Robert W Powers were both awarded DFCs for hitting the target, despite heavy flak. Another series of raids involving all three groups was staged on 26 March, when the wing returned to the Arezzo viaduct. As with previous missions against this target, the bombers failed to hit the viaduct, although crews from the 320th did destroy a repair train and cut the tracks.

Brig Gen R M Webster, Commanding General of the 42nd BW, observed the bombing on this mission from a 444th BS Marauder.

On 27 March the 17th and 319th BGs missed the Poggibonsi railway bridges, with the latter group having attempted to hit the Incisa bridge – all 26 of its Marauders missed the target!

Two days later, FFAF squadron 1/22 'Maroc', attached to the 17th BG at Villacidro, flew its first mission when it bombed the docks on the Italian islands of Elba. Prior to performing this operation, the FFAF had sent its USAAF-trained Marauder crews to observe earlier missions conducted by the 42nd BW. There would eventually be six FFAF-manned B-26 units assigned to the 42nd BW.

The 319th BG flew its 200th mission on 1 April when the group again attacked the Incisa railway bridge. Bombs exploded all around the structure, but they missed the target. The 320th BG returned to Incisa six days later, when 23 of its B-26s dropped 91 1000-lb demolition bombs and scored both direct hits and near misses on the bridge, and possible direct hits on the viaduct. The bridge was, at least, finally destroyed.

Some 24 B-26s of the 320th BG returned to the Bucine viaducts on 10 April, although cloud obscured the target on the first bomb run. Forced to make a second pass, the formation scored at least one direct hit on the centre of the viaduct. The group attacked Bucine again on the 14th, when 17 of its 24 Marauders dropped their bombs on both the north and south viaducts. Crews put a good concentration of bombs in the target area, damaging the railway lines but missing both viaducts. The rest of the formation returned with their bombs, as they were not in the correct position to drop.

That same day the 319th BG attempted to hit the Poggibonsi, Certaldo and Cecina railway bridges, but missed all three.

Following the widening of the runway at Decimomannu, the 319th BG conducted its first six-ship take-off on 20 April 1944. The flight leaders launched slightly ahead of their two wing ships – in this instance, B-26C-45 42-107565 B/N 88 *Roger The Dodger* and B-26B-30 41-31969 B/N 96 *Ruth Marie* lead the unidentified Marauder nearest to the camera, together with B-26C-45 42-107561 B/N 97 *Tally Ho*, B-26B-50 B/N 77 42-95955 and B-26B-50 B/N 89 42-95983, all which were assigned to the 440th BS. Axis fighters shot down *Roger The Dodger* and *Tally Ho*, together with B-26C-20–MO 41-35041 B/N 93, on 19 October 1944 during an attack on the railway bridge at Mantua (*Louise Hertenstein*)

On 20 April the 319th BG staged its first six-aircraft take-off from Decimomannu following the completion of runway widening work. The group headed to the Poggibonsi railway bridge and viaduct once again, but due to cloud over the objective, crews bombed their alternate target – the Leghorn (Livorno) railway marshalling yard – instead.

The 320th BG also staged its first multi-aircraft take-off from Decimomannu on the 20th when it despatched four B-26s at a time and sent them to bomb the viaducts at Bucine and Arezzo. The weather prevented the group from reaching the target, and they turned back at Cecina. Flying a Marauder on the latter mission was 2Lt John Malcolm of the 441st BS, who recalled;

'With the end of the rainy season, our airstrip was improved, but now we were faced with a new problem – dust. We were using 15-second intervals between our aeroplanes when taking off, but this did not cure the problem. Despite this gap, often, after the first aeroplane had taken off, it was almost "instrument conditions" for the pilot of the next bomber in the line. And things just got progressively worse with each aircraft that departed.

'There were two B-26 groups operating from Decimomannu, namely the 319th and 320th BGs. The latter group adopted a four-aeroplane abreast take-off procedure which practically eliminated the dust problem. It also improved our formation join up time and bomb pattern. The 319th went two better, managing to send off six B-26s at a time in a line abreast formation.

'I really loved this change because the join up for the formation could now be performed quickly, and you could also fly much closer together. Flying our new landing pattern was also great fun too. We would come in for a landing in flights of four in echelon, and as the pilot in the lead ship reached the end of the approach runway, he would drop the gear and flaps and commence a steep turn into the runway. The three remaining aircraft then peeled off at ten-second intervals, using the same procedure. Flying fighter style approaches proved very popular with us bomber pilots, and greatly cut down the amount of dust swirling around over the field too.

'Another practice we instituted in our squadron was to check out the co-pilots as first pilots, which soon meant that we had more pilots than crews. The solution to this "problem" was to pair up two newly checked out pilots, who would then alternate positions during the course of a combat mission. I was teamed up with 2Lt Robert Wilson, but the partnership only lasted for three missions – I believe operations decided we were not made for each other!

'On our first mission together, the hydraulics system was knocked out by flak. This proved to be no real problem, since the B-26's emergency air brake worked well. On our second mission we had some other minor problem, but our third mission I remember vividly. It was a rough day, not only for us, but for many other crews as well. The flak was very heavy, and I think our aeroplane got hit by most of it. We were really shot up, and our bombardier was killed. We made an emergency landing at an airfield on Corsica so that the bombardier could receive medical care, but we were too late. We flew back to Sardinia, and after we landed I recall looking over the aeroplane. Not only were there a lot of flak holes, one shot had almost severed the walkway that ran from the bomb-bay to the tail gunner's position.'

The mission mentioned by 2Lt Malcolm, which was flown on 22 April, had seen the 320th BG targeting both the Poggibonsi and Incisa railway bridges once again. As he related, the flak proved to be particularly accurate, and 27 of the group's 48 Marauders were damaged, killing one airman and wounding fifteen others. Bombardier TSgt Rodney H Blackford had suffered mortal wounds when hit by a piece of shrapnel whilst his aircraft (B-26C-45 42-95761 B/N 10 *Miss Elaine*, flown by Flt Off Robert V Wilson) was on its bomb run. B-26B-45 42-95791 B/N 7 *Sweet and Low*, flown by 1Lt Augusta L West, returned on one engine with seriously injured co-pilot 2Lt Ray L Arnsdorff. West was awarded a DFC for his actions, but *Sweet and Low* was destroyed in the crash-landing on Corsica. Despite the best efforts of the 320th BG, the bridges at Poggibonsi and Incisa were still standing.

22 April also saw the 319th BG target both the Poggibonsi viaduct and the Tabianello north railway bridge. During the bomb run, the Marauders had to dive to avoid a 17th BG formation that was in the process of hitting a stretch of railway line between Incisa and Valdorno. Later flights did, however, confirm definite hits on the Tabianello bridge.

The 320th BG missed the Poggibonsi bridge once again on 23 April, but it did succeed in cutting its approach lines at either end. That same day, both the 17th and 319th BGs again attacked the Incisa railway bridge and viaduct, and the latter group returned to this target 24 hours later, scoring some direct hits. The 320th BG continued the campaign against the targets at Incisa, flying four missions between 25 and 30 April, but more attacks would be needed before the wing could claim their destruction.

During the same period, the 319th BG had some success against another difficult target – the railway bridges and viaducts near Arezzo. On

This photograph, although of poor quality, shows the separation between each Marauder. In the event of power loss or a blown tyre, there was enough room for a Marauder to swerve inside the other aeroplanes in the flight. Taking off in six-ship formations cut 25 minutes off the group's join up times. The 320th BG often flew four-ship flights, thus limiting the number of B-26s it could launch at once (*Louise Hertenstein*)

25 April, the group attacked the railway bridge two-and-a-half miles west of the city, but cloud prevented half of the Marauders from dropping their bombs. The target was missed, but one flight of three B-26s dropped on the Asciano bridge instead, as this was the alternate target. A good concentration of bombs possibly cut one of its approach lines.

Returning to the railway bridge just east of Arezzo on 28 April, the 319th scored some direct hits. It again hit the Arezzo targets two days later, and this time scored direct hits on both the bridges and the viaducts. Elsewhere that same day, the 17th BG bombed a railway bridge at Cortona, claiming two hits and cutting the tracks.

On 1 May the 17th BG targeted the railway bridge at Pescaia, whilst the 319th BG sent 36 Marauders in two 18-aircraft formations to the Campo di Marte railway marshalling yards in Florence. The weather intervened, so two formations of nine B-26s attacked alternate targets – the Pontedera railway bridge and the Califura railway viaduct. Results on the first target were not seen due to cloud cover and smoke from an attack conducted moments before by the 320th BG. Extensive damage was inflicted on the railway viaduct, however.

The 319th BG's second 18-aeroplane formation also had trouble seeing the target, and only one flight dropped accurately on the railway marshalling yards. Unfortunately, some of the bombs also fell on surrounding buildings. During the course of this mission, 1Lt Elliot Lysco's mount, B-26B-10 41-18322 B/N 64 *Hell's Belle II*, became the first Marauder to fly 100 missions in the MTO.

The group returned to Campo di Marte the next day, with all the formations hitting the target. 437th BS B-26B-50 42-96011, flown by 1Lt William 'Spec' Young, crash-landed with an engine out at Ghisonaccia, on the east coast of Corsica, killing both the pilot and gunner SSgt John Santa.

The final ten days of *Strangle* began with another attack against the railway marshalling yards at Florence, conducted by both the 17th and 320th BGs, followed by an attack by the former group on the Ventimiglia railway marshalling yards the following day. The wing then hit either bridges or viaducts at Arezzo, Borgo San Lorenzo, Certaldo, Imperia, Incisa, Poggibonsi, San Giovanni and Ventimiglia.

B-26C-11-MO 41-18322 B/N 64 *Hell's Belle II* of the 439th BS/319th BG taxies out at the start of its 101st mission, having become the first USAAF bomber to reach the century mark on 1 May 1944 when it participated in an attack on the Campo di Marte railway marshalling yards in Florence. The Marauder completed a total of 132 missions with the group prior to being retired (*Author*)

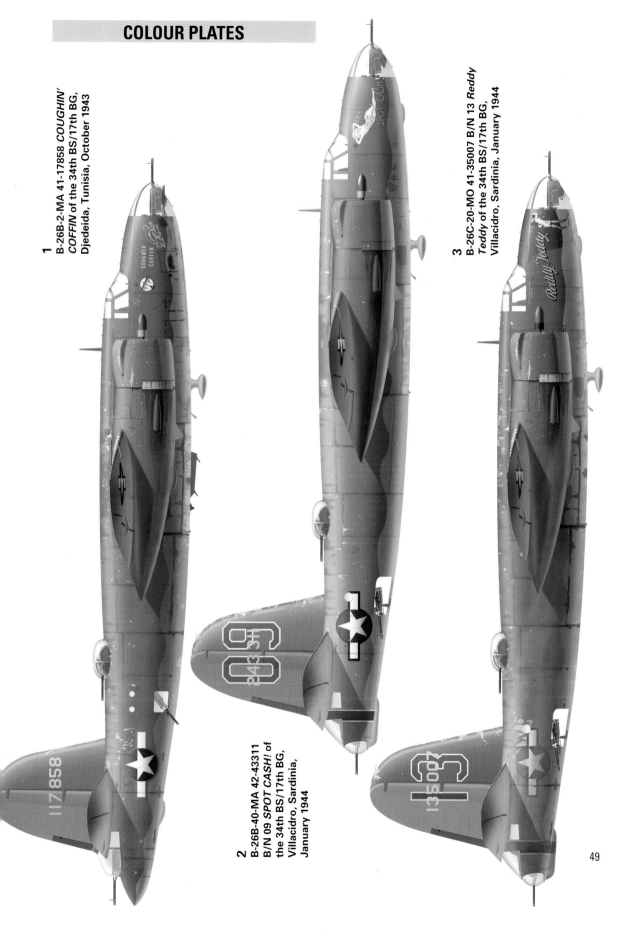

1
B-26B-2-MA 41-17858 *COUGHIN'*
COFFIN of the 34th BS/17th BG,
Djedeida, Tunisia, October 1943

2
B-26B-40-MA 42-43311
B/N 09 *SPOT CASH!* of
the 34th BS/17th BG,
Villacidro, Sardinia,
January 1944

3
B-26C-20-MO 41-35007 B/N 13 *Reddy*
Teddy of the 34th BS/17th BG,
Villacidro, Sardinia, January 1944

49

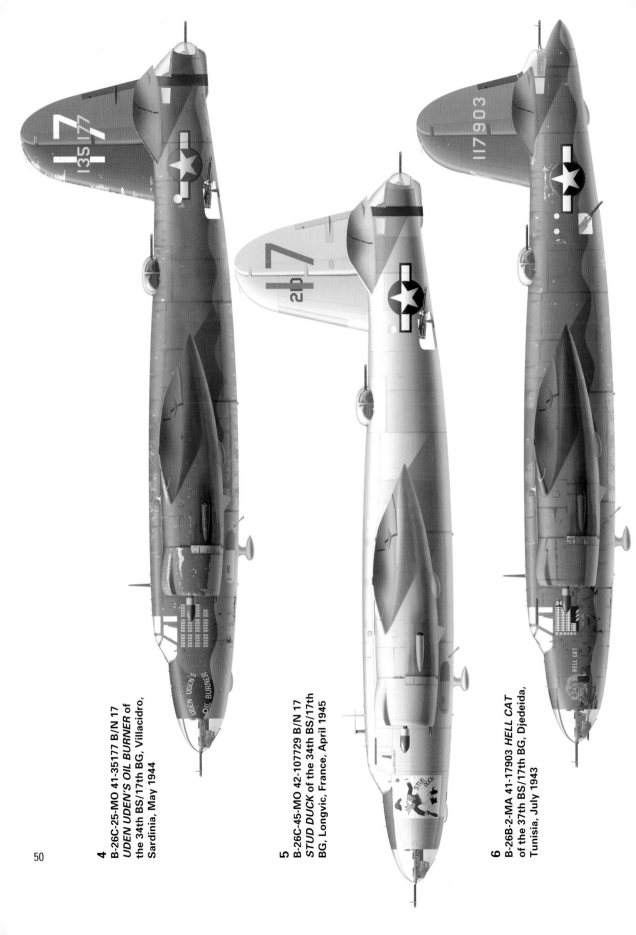

4
B-26C-25-MO 41-35177 B/N 17
UDEN UDEN'S OIL BURNER of
the 34th BS/17th BG, Villacidro,
Sardinia, May 1944

5
B-26C-45-MO 42-107729 B/N 17
STUD DUCK of the 34th BS/17th
BG, Longvic, France, April 1945

6
B-26B-2-MA 41-17903 *HELL CAT*
of the 37th BS/17th BG, Djedeida,
Tunisia, July 1943

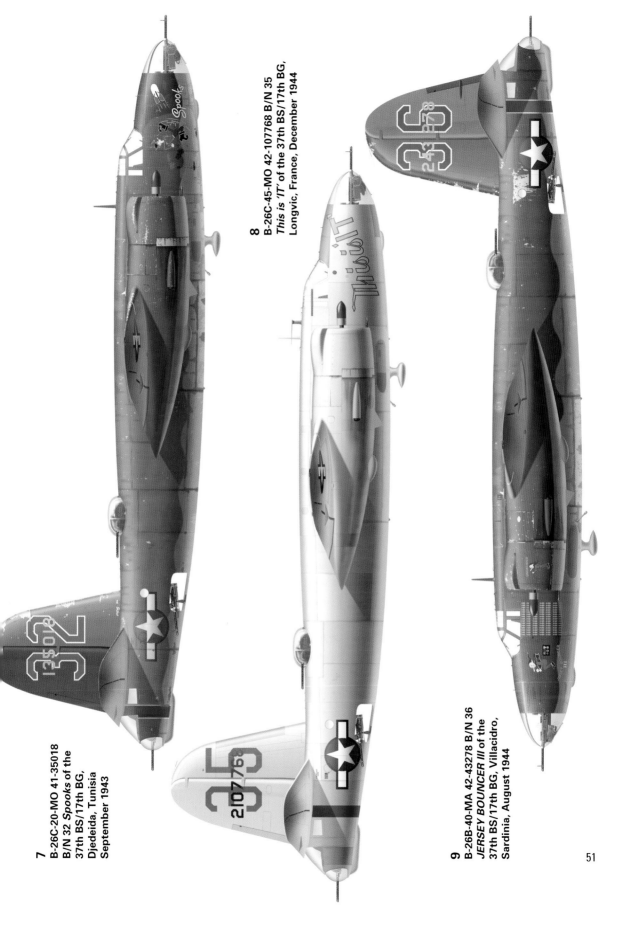

7
B-26C-20-MO 41-35018
B/N 32 *Spooks* of the
37th BS/17th BG,
Djedeida, Tunisia
September 1943

8
B-26C-45-MO 42-107768 B/N 35
This is 'IT' of the 37th BS/17th BG,
Longvic, France, December 1944

9
B-26B-40-MA 42-43278 B/N 36
JERSEY BOUNCER III of the
37th BS/17th BG, Villacidro,
Sardinia, August 1944

51

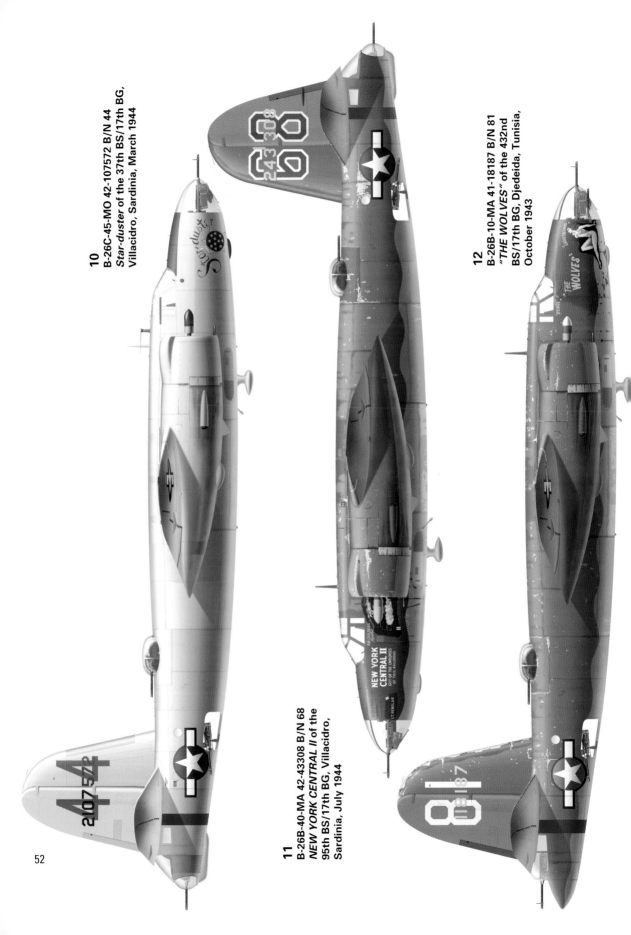

10
B-26C-45-MO 42-107572 B/N 44
Star-duster of the 37th BS/17th BG,
Villacidro, Sardinia, March 1944

11
B-26B-40-MA 42-43308 B/N 68
NEW YORK CENTRAL II of the
95th BS/17th BG, Villacidro,
Sardinia, July 1944

12
B-26B-10-MA 41-18187 B/N 81
"THE WOLVES" of the 432nd
BS/17th BG, Djedeida, Tunisia,
October 1943

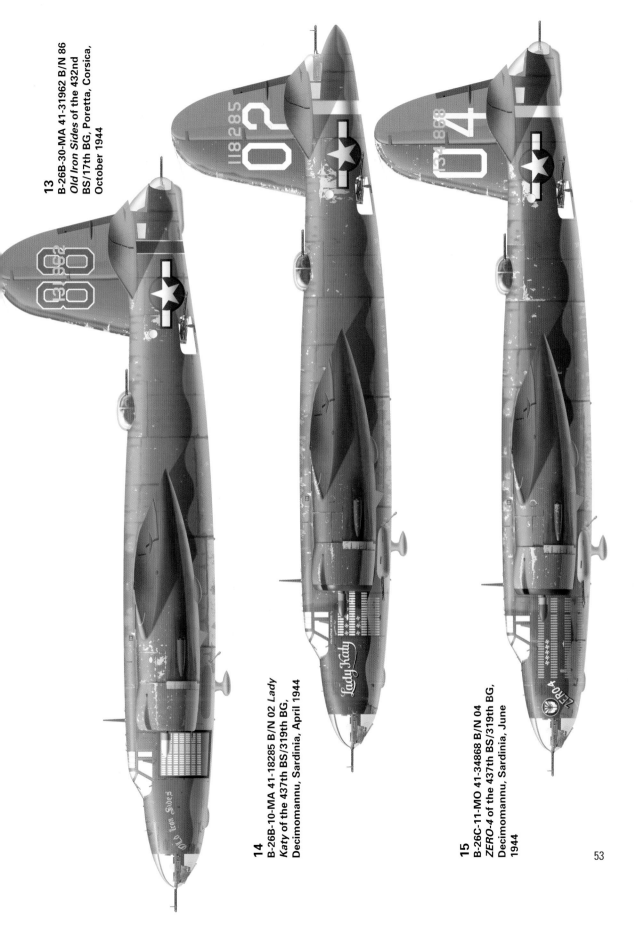

13
B-26B-30-MA 41-31962 B/N 86
Old Iron Sides of the 432nd
BS/17th BG, Poretta, Corsica,
October 1944

14
B-26B-10-MA 41-18285 B/N 02 *Lady
Katy* of the 437th BS/319th BG,
Decimomannu, Sardinia, April 1944

15
B-26C-11-MO 41-34868 B/N 04
ZERO-4 of the 437th BS/319th BG,
Decimomannu, Sardinia, June
1944

53

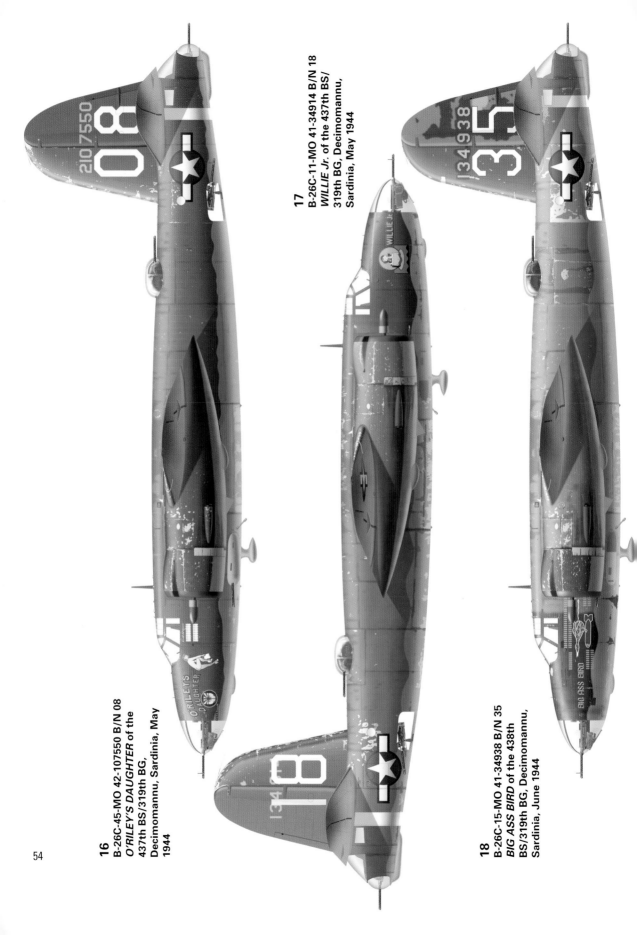

16
B-26C-45-MO 42-107550 B/N 08
O'RILEY'S DAUGHTER of the
437th BS/319th BG,
Decimomannu, Sardinia, May
1944

17
B-26C-11-MO 41-34914 B/N 18
WILLIE Jr. of the 437th BS/
319th BG, Decimomannu,
Sardinia, May 1944

18
B-26C-15-MO 41-34938 B/N 35
BIG ASS BIRD of the 438th
BS/319th BG, Decimomannu,
Sardinia, June 1944

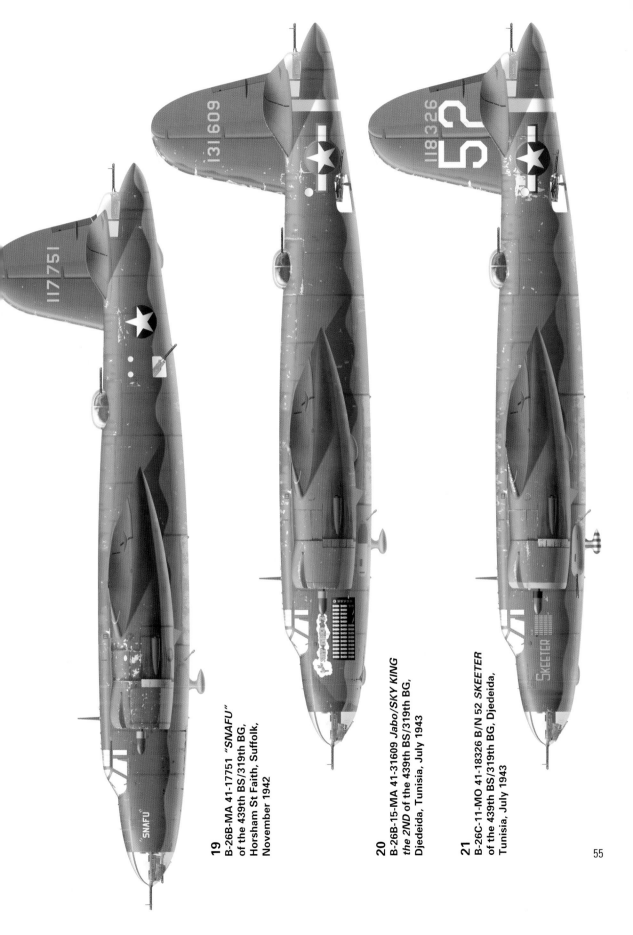

19
B-26B-MA 41-17751 *"SNAFU"*
of the 439th BS/319th BG,
Horsham St Faith, Suffolk,
November 1942

20
B-26B-15-MA 41-31609 *Jabo/SKY KING
the 2ND* of the 439th BS/319th BG,
Djedeida, Tunisia, July 1943

21
B-26C-11-MO 41-18326 B/N 52 *SKEETER*
of the 439th BS/319th BG, Djedeida,
Tunisia, July 1943

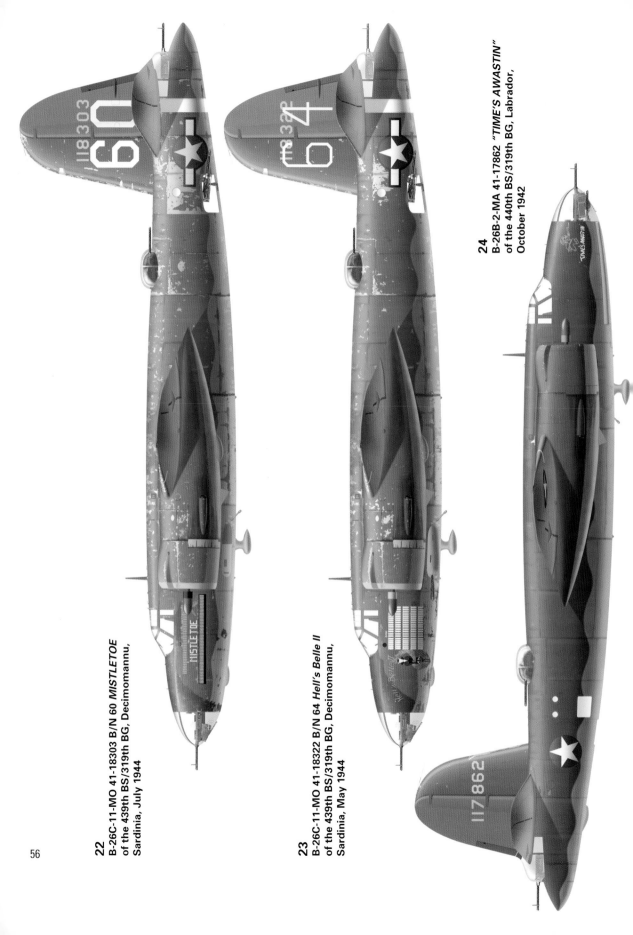

22
B-26C-11-MO 41-18303 B/N 60 *MISTLETOE*
of the 439th BS/319th BG, Decimomannu,
Sardinia, July 1944

23
B-26C-11-MO 41-18322 B/N 64 *Hell's Belle II*
of the 439th BS/319th BG, Decimomannu,
Sardinia, May 1944

24
B-26B-2-MA 41-17862 *"TIME'S AWASTIN"*
of the 440th BS/319th BG, Labrador,
October 1942

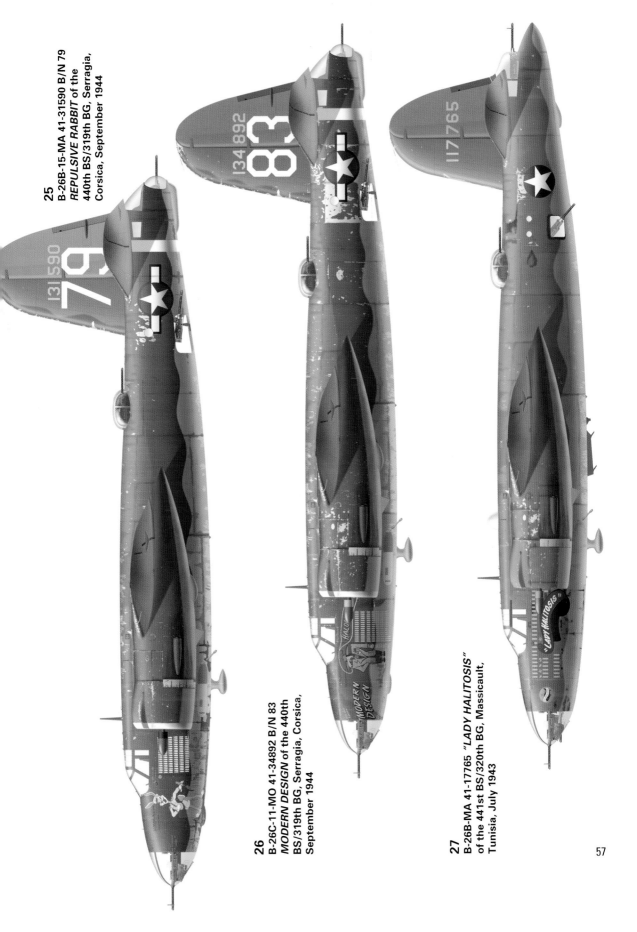

25
B-26B-15-MA 41-31590 B/N 79
REPULSIVE RABBIT of the
440th BS/319th BG, Serragia,
Corsica, September 1944

26
B-26C-11-MO 41-34892 B/N 83
MODERN DESIGN of the 440th
BS/319th BG, Serragia, Corsica,
September 1944

27
B-26B-MA 41-17765 *"LADY HALITOSIS"*
of the 441st BS/320th BG, Massicault,
Tunisia, July 1943

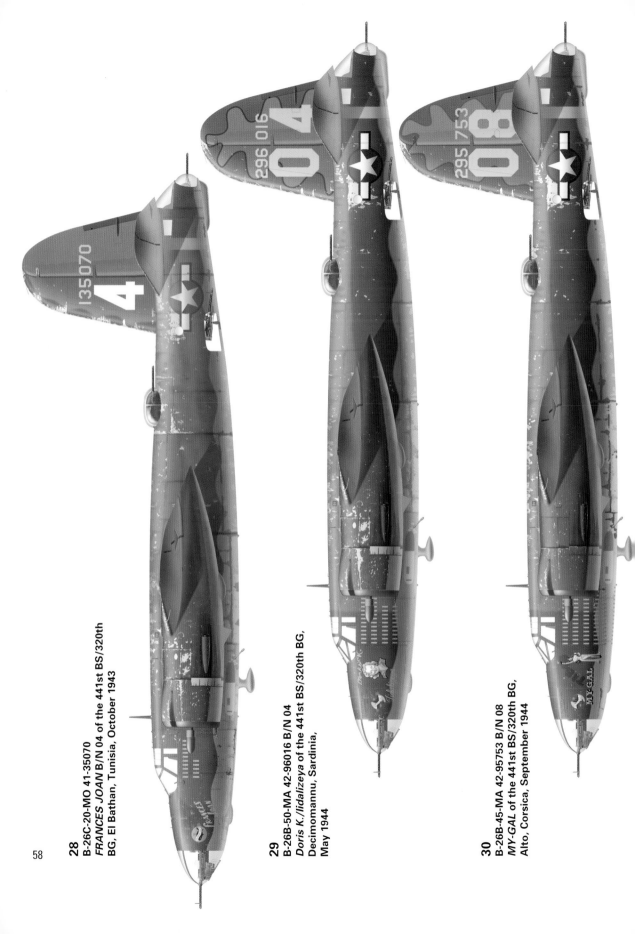

28
B-26C-20-MO 41-35070
FRANCES JOAN B/N 04 of the 441st BS/320th
BG, El Bathan, Tunisia, October 1943

29
B-26B-50-MA 42-96016 B/N 04
Doris K./lidalizeya of the 441st BS/320th BG,
Decimomannu, Sardinia,
May 1944

30
B-26B-45-MA 42-95753 B/N 08
MY-GAL of the 441st BS/320th BG,
Alto, Corsica, September 1944

31
B-26B-10-MA 41-18305 B/N 14
Miss Manchester of the 441st BS/320th BG,
Decimomannu, Sardinia, December 1943

32
B-26G-5-MA 43-34284 B/N 32
Green Eyed Glodine of the 442nd BS/320th BG,
Longvic, France, January 1945

33
B-26C-20-MO 41-34999 B/N 33
"SHIF'LESS" of the 442nd BS/320th BG,
Decimomannu, Sardinia, February 1944

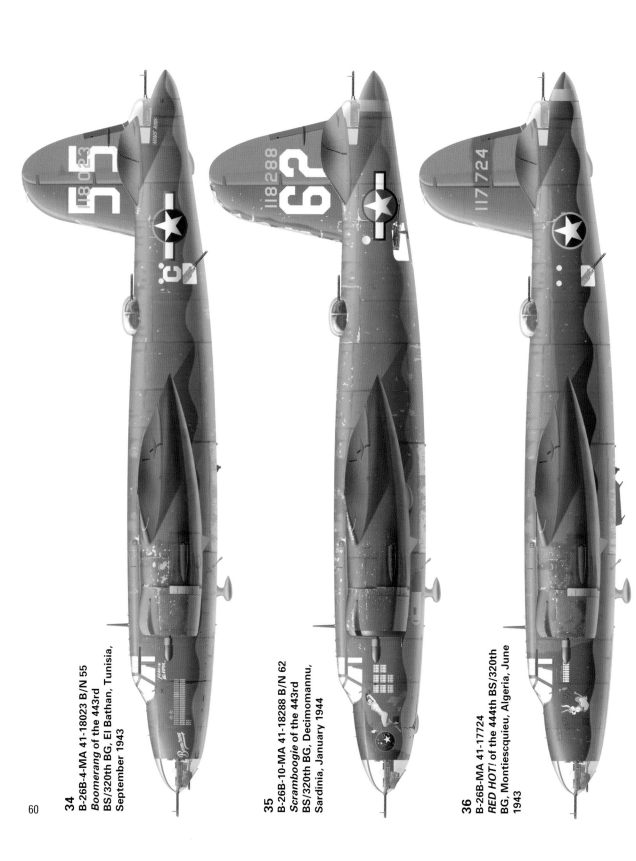

34
B-26B-4-MA 41-18023 B/N 55
Boomerang of the 443rd
BS/320th BG, El Bathan, Tunisia,
September 1943

35
B-26B-10-MA 41-18288 B/N 62
Scramboogie of the 443rd
BS/320th BG, Decimomannu,
Sardinia, January 1944

36
B-26B-MA 41-17724
RED HOT! of the 444th BS/320th
BG, Montiescquieu, Algeria, June
1943

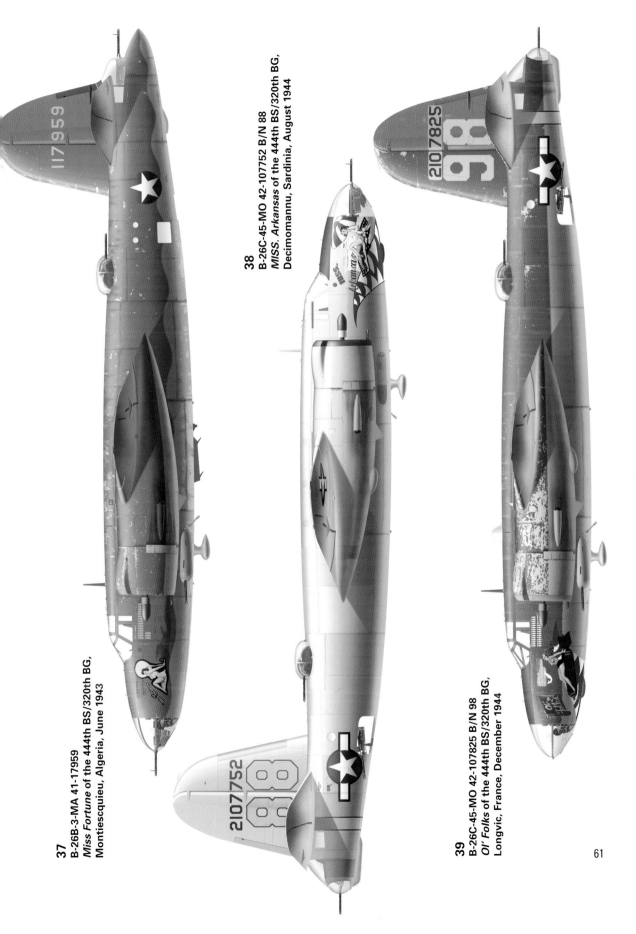

37
B-26B-3-MA 41-17959
Miss Fortune of the 444th BS/320th BG,
Montiesquieu, Algeria, June 1943

38
B-26C-45-MO 42-107752 B/N 88
MISS. Arkansas of the 444th BS/320th BG,
Decimomannu, Sardinia, August 1944

39
B-26C-45-MO 42-107825 B/N 98
Ol' Folks of the 444th BS/320th BG,
Longvic, France, December 1944

ON THE ATTACK

Operation *Diadem* was launched on 12 May 1944 when the US Fifth and British Eighth Armies broke through the enemy's 'Winter Line', thus allowing Allied troops to move up into the Liri Valley and onto Rome. The operation was timed to roughly coincide with the planned invasion of France in an effort to tie down German forces that might otherwise have been used to repel the Normandy landings. Allied bombers would play a crucial role in *Diadem* by targeting communication lines, supply routes and the Wehrmacht's ability to withdraw troops to the 'Gothic Line'.

On 12 May the 42nd BW made its first contribution to the success of the campaign by attacking German troop concentrations in Pontecorvo and Fondi. This mission saw the 319th BG introduce a new way of delivering its bombs, as developed by acting group bombardier 1Lt Shu. The bomb fuses were timed so that the weapons exploded 150 ft to 300 ft above the ground, with the resulting fragmentation proving deadly to enemy personnel within range of the blast pattern.

Some 44 B-26s from the 319th were involved in this mission, and the flak was heavy – no fewer than 32 Marauders were damaged and two 438th BS aircraft brought down. One of the aeroplanes lost was the unit's lead ship, B-26B-50 42-95888, flown by Capt Robert H Wilson. On board was the 438th BS CO Maj Jack M Yates, who was taken prisoner but later escaped. Before heading home, he briefly returned to the unit in June and gave lectures to the group on effective escape techniques. The other aeroplane shot down by flak that day was B-26B-40 42-43300, flown by 1Lt Dowaine C Daniels.

Reports from the battlefield revealed that the Germans had lost a lot of men during the attacks on 12 May, and this confirmed the effectiveness of 1Lt Shu's short-fused bombs against troops in the open.

The 320th BG had also seen action over Fondi on the 12th, and the group was awarded a DUC for 'pressing home its attacks on enemy troop concentrations in the face of an intense anti-aircraft barrage'.

The 319th targeted a railway bridge northwest of Montepescali the following day, and yet another Marauder was lost. B-26B-10 41-18263 B/N 55 *Duration Plus* was heading out on its 99th mission when it suffered a runaway propeller whilst taking off. The bomber ran off the end of the runway and exploded, injuring several members of its crew. The remaining aircraft in the group missed the bridge, but succeeded in cutting the tracks in three places.

Over the next ten days, the 42nd BW attacked road and railway bridges at Arezzo, Calafuria, Castro di Volsci, Ceprano, Certaldo, Fontana Liri, Grizzana, Lissono, Pisa, Poggibonsi, Pontedera, San Giovanni, Tabianello and Vado. During this period, the Marauders introduced chaff (tin foil cut into strips and dropped in bundles in flight in an effort to confuse enemy radar) for the first time. The 319th BG used chaff for the first time when it attacked the Fontana Liri road bridge on 21 May. Its

The first production Marauders had provision for a flexible 0.30-cal machine gun installed in the upper half of the Plexiglas nose cone, which was operated by the bombardier. From the B-26B-4 model onwards, a more powerful 0.50-cal machine gun could be mounted in the tip of the nose cone. The Marauder's nose cone was strengthened in the B-10, and all subsequent models, through the addition of two bracing frames in the upper section of the Plexiglas, which are clearly visible in this photograph. When not in use, the gun was swung to one side and retained in place by a thin 'banjo' wire attached to the fuselage. Only lead ships carried a Norden bombsight, with toggeliers in the wing ships dropping their bombs on the direction of the lead bombardier (*Louise Hertenstein*)

Marauders of the 319th BG fly close formation. Wing ships would fly very close to the flight leaders on the bomb run, often having their wings overlapping. Note the glass panel fitted to the single-piece rear bomb-bay doors in the B-26 in the foreground. A strike camera could be located in this position. In practice most strike photos were taken using hand-held cameras in the waist positions. Originally, the rear bomb-bay could house up to 4800-lb of smaller bombs. Following its lack of use in combat, Martin sealed the rear doors shut from the B-26B-20 onwards and fitted two 250-gallon fuel tanks in the bay instead. The rear bomb-bay doors differed from the centrally hinging two-piece forward bay doors, and were totally deleted from B-40 model onwards (*Louise Hertenstein*)

B-26C-15 41-34938 B/N 35 *BIG ASS BIRD* of the 438th BS flew its 100th mission when it led the 319th BG against troop concentrations in the Albano and Ariccia areas on 1 June 1944. Ultimately completing 145 missions (the highest number for a 319th BG B-26), it was retired in November 1944 (*Louise Hertenstein*)

effectiveness as a defensive measure was initially difficult to determine, as it was assumed that there was little, if any, radar-controlled flak in the area – 12 B-26s were shot up nonetheless. The 319th BG dropped a good concentration of bombs in the target area, but crews missed the bridge.

Allied ground forces achieved rapid gains at the start of *Diadem*, and the 'Gustav Line' soon began to collapse. Cassino was finally captured on 20 May following a seven-month battle, and German troops fell back on the 'Hitler Line', some ten miles further north. The wing continued its support of the offensive by attacking both rail and road targets in the Liri Valley, thus hampering the German withdrawal.

The ground fighting had also drawn in German reserves, which in turn relieved the pressure on battle-weary Allied troops at Anzio and allowed them to finally break out and begin their advance northwards on 23 May.

The Marauder units concentrated on the roads for a few days during this period, with their targets primarily being junctions. Crews used their bombs to crater the roads, thereby making them temporarily impassable. Targets included roads in Anagni, Carsoli, Ferentino, Genzano, Marine, Moletta, Roviano, Subiaco, Valmontone Velletri and Viterbo.

On 23 May, the 17th BG introduced chaff for the first time when it bombed the Marine road junction. None of the B-26s involved in the mission were damaged by flak, but the formation was set upon by 15 fighters. The Marauders flew into cloud and escaped, sustaining no losses.

Over the next 72 hours, the 42nd BW again attacked bridges, this time at Arezzo, Borghetto, Catiglion Fiorentino, Compiobbi, Cortona, Ladispoli, Monterotondo, Narni, Poggibonsi, Pontassieve, Spoleto, Stifone, Torrita Savina, Torrita di Siena, Terni and Terentola. Then, on 31 May and 1 June, German troops were hit at Albano, Ariccia, Genazzano, Palestrina and Pisoniano. The mission to Albano and Ariccia on 1 June was led by 319th BG B-26C-15 41-34938 B/N 35 *BIG ASS BIRD*, which was flying its 100th mission.

Gen Mark Clark's Fifth Army liberated Rome on 3 June, and by concentrating on taking the Italian capital, the Allies allowed the bulk of the German 10th Army to retreat northwards firstly to the 'Trasimene Line' and then on to the 'Gothic Line'. Enemy troops were attacked throughout their 240-mile retreat by the pursuing British Eighth Army.

The 42nd BW assisted British forces in their efforts to hinder the enemy's withdrawal by attacking bridges during the first two weeks of June. The three groups targeted bridges at or near Acqualagna, Albinia, Amelia, Arezzo, Attigliano, Baschi, Borghetto, Bucine, Cagli, Castiglion Fiorentino, Cecina, Civita Castellana, Collepepe, Farmignano, Ficulle, Foligno, Montepescali, Narni, Orvieto, Perugia, Pesaro, Piteccio, Pode Nuovo, Poggibonsi, Pontassieve, Radiocofani, Rieti, Roccastrada, Siena, Spoleto, Staz di Ficulle, Tabianello, Terni, Todi, Vetralla and Viterbo.

Enjoying a break from 'bridge busting', the 319th and 320th BGs flew some unusual missions to Leghorn harbour on 13 June. The

Germans were preparing to scuttle two cement-filled ships in the harbour mouth in order to prevent its use by the Allies, and the groups were tasked with sinking the vessels before they reached their intended positions. Both units despatched 18 Marauders, with the 319th BG attacking first using RDX (one of the most powerful of all non-nuclear high explosives) bombs. Its crews scored direct hits on one ship and near misses on the other, and the 320th BG formation that followed saw a vessel burning and the other one sinking. The next day, the 319th BG sortied another 18 aeroplanes to finish off the ships.

Crew names are added to the nose area of B-26C-10 41-34868 B/N 04 *ZERO-4* of the 437th BS/319th BG. The nearest name on the nose gear door is that of the aeroplane's crew chief, SSgt Leo E Walker II. *ZERO-4* completed its 100th mission on 6 June 1944, and went on to tally 148 missions prior to being flown back to the US by Capt Richard C Bushee that November. *ZERO-4* flew 25 times as group leader, 53 times as flight leader and 24 times as an element leader. The bomber also had 13 engine changes during its frontline career (*Louise Hertenstein*)

On 14 June the British Eighth Army finally captured two of the wing's more difficult targets, Orvietto and Terni. That same day the first of three non-operational tragedies occurred that would affect each of the three groups over the next 72 hours.

17th BG B-26B-50 42-95954 B/N 05 of the 34th BS, flown by 1Lt John E Lee, went down in the Mediterranean after suffering an engine failure. Searches were mounted but no survivors were found. All 12 personnel on board were presumed killed, including six Red Cross nurses being ferried to Sardinia from Italy for a dance.

The next day Capt Art Riegel of the 319th BG buzzed the bathing beach at Cagliari, on Sardinia, and crashed when he came in too low and his B-26 (serial unknown) clipped a telegraph pole. The aeroplane crashed and exploded, killing the pilot and five of his crew. Riegel had flown 72 missions and was soon to rotate home.

Then, on 17 June, B-26B-50 42-96022 B/N 19 *BOBO The Strong Boy* of the 441st BS/320th BG also went down in the Mediterranean close to Sardinia whilst on a flight from Oran. The bomber, crewed by pilot 1Lt George 'Jack' Dillon, co-pilot Flt Off Elwin Goodenough and bombardier TSgt William McFarland, was ferrying 16 FFAF personnel to Sardinia. All three groups searched for survivors seen floating in rafts, but the weather quickly deteriorated and the men were never seen again.

During the final days of Operation *Diadem*, which ended on 22 June, through to month-end, the wing hit road and rail bridges at Arezzo, Bucine, Castelecchio di Reno, Castelnuova Serivia, Castiglioncello, Lissono, Massa, Pisa, Pontremoli, Recco, Rignano, Rimini, Vergato, Viareggio, Villafranca and Zoagli. The strike on the latter target, conducted on 20 June, was another exceptional 100 per cent mission flown by the 17th BG, whose crews destroyed a railway viaduct.

The success of this operation contrasted markedly with a mission flown three days earlier by the 319th BG, which had been sent to bomb a railway bridge at Rimini. There was cause for concern at Decimomannu when none of the aeroplanes returned to base and nothing was heard from them, despite the bombers being more than two hours overdue. It

B-26B-50 42-96022 B/N 19 *BOBO The Strong Boy* of the 441st BS/ 320th BG was one of four 42nd BW Marauders that were lost in non-operational accidents over a four-day period between 14-17 June 1944, resulting in the death of 31 service personnel. *BOBO The Strong Boy* was the last of these aircraft to be lost when it crashed into the sea 40 miles off Sardinia on the 17th. The 320th launched 29 B-26s between 1255 hrs on the 17th and 0044 hrs on the 18th as it searched for survivors. On the 17th, one of the bombers spotted three men in the water and dropped additional life rafts and vests. During daylight hours on the 18th, another 16 B-26s were launched and searched all day long, but saw nothing. On 19 June, 14 B-26s continued the search, and a crew spotted empty life rafts and vests, but no survivors. The B-26's three crew and fifteen passengers had perished (*via Franz Reisdorf*)

B-26B-40 42-43278 B/N 36 *JERSEY BOUNCER III* of the 37th BS/17th BG was the first Marauder in this group to complete 100 missions. It went on to fly 130 missions prior to being shot down over the 'Siegfried Line' on 17 December 1944. Cartoon characters adorned both sides of the nose, as well as both engines (*Alf Egil Johannessen*)

transpired that both group formations could not find the target due to poor weather, so they had diverted to the Fifteenth Air Force base at Amendola (one of the Marauders had landed at nearby Foggia) to refuel and then try again.

Mission Commander 439th BS CO Maj Harold G Senften duly led 31 B-26s from Amendola to the secondary target – the railway bridges southeast of Siena. Again, cloud stymied the group's attack runs, so the bombers gave up and returned to Sardinia.

Bad weather continued to hamper missions during this period, and none were successfully carried out for a whole week. Then, on 29 June, all three groups were back in action, allowing the 17th BG to fly its 300th mission of the war when it attacked the ammunition dumps at La Spezia. Three days later, on a mission to the Vado railway viaduct, the group's veteran B-26B-40 42-43278 B/N 36 *JERSEY BOUNCER III* became the first 17th BG Marauder to complete 100 missions – group CO Col Donald L Gilbert flew as its co-pilot on this sortie.

During the first 11 days of July, the three groups attacked bridges at or near Borgo Val di Taro, Fidenza, Fiorenzuola, Marzabotto, Peteccio, Piacenza, Pontremoli, Prato, Ronco Scrivia, Vado Ligure and Villafranca. There were, however, other types of targets being hit as well, with fuel depots/storage tanks and ammunition factories all being visited by Marauders from the 42nd BW.

With the Germans in retreat and their defences in disarray, few USAAF bombers were now being brought down by flak or fighters. The one exception to this rule came on 10 July, when the railway bridge north of Marzabotto was attacked. Crews were surprised by the ferocity and accuracy of the flak defending this target, and four B-26s were damaged and one brought down. The latter aircraft, B-26C-45 42-107566 B/N 06 of the 441st BS/320th BG, was on its bomb run when it was hit by at least one 88 mm shell. The round damaged the bomber's fin and left horizontal stabiliser and tore off the left wing outboard of the engine. Pilot 1Lt Murray B Wiginton Jr fought to control the aeroplane by pulling full aileron deflection on the right wing, but the bomber immediately started to spin, trapping the six-man crew – no one survived.

Wiginton and his co-pilot, 2Lt William E Wigginton, were not related, but they had requested to fly all their missions together. Exploration of the crash site during the 1980s discovered Wiginton's dog tags and the remains of radio/gunner Sgt Wesley B Hoffman, who was reburied in the Arlington National Cemetery on 1 October 1991.

MAJOR MALLORY

Staged between the 12 and 14 July, Operation *Major Mallory* was a successful attempt to destroy the bridges over the Po River. Targets were located at Casalmaggiore, Cremona, Guastalla, Piacenza and Viadana. In response to this offensive, the Germans started using smoke pots to try and obscure the bridges in the hope that the bombardiers would not be

On 10 July 1944, during a mission to the railway bridge north of Marzabotto, B-26C-45 42-107566 B/N 06 of the 441st BS/320th BG was hit in the left wing by at least one 88 mm shell. In this dramatic photograph, it can be seen that the aircraft's pilot, 1Lt Murray B Wiginton Jr, pulled on full aileron deflection on the right wing in an effort to control the aeroplane as it began to spin to the left. Note that the bomber has also lost a portion of its fin and left horizontal stabiliser as well. Wiginton and his crew, namely co-pilot 2Lt William E Wigginton, bombardier Pfc Norford G Meador, engineer Sgt Earnest D Casey, radio/gunner SSgt Wesley B Hoffman and SSgt Philip A Iannotta, were unable to escape from the wildly spinning aircraft prior to it hitting the ground. Wiginton and co-pilot Wigginton were not related, but they had requested to fly all their missions together (*Chuck O'Mahony*)

able to aim their ordnance properly. Occasionally, this tactic worked, but the 42nd BW soon developed its own ways to deal with the pots.

Wind direction was taken into account during mission planning, and target bomb runs were changed so as to minimise the effect of the smoke. Bombardiers were also thoroughly briefed on the target surroundings so that, if necessary, they could estimate its exact location if totally obscured. The lack of defences in the form of fighters and flak also allowed the wing to make longer, stable, bomb runs directly at the target without having to deviate to throw off the aim of flak gunners or enemy pilots. Such attack profiles greatly enhanced accuracy.

The 17th BG's first *Major Mallory* target was the railway bridge at Piacenza. Constructed of steel, it would prove difficult to destroy. The group flew two missions to the bridge on the 12th, but it would take a lot more bombs to ensure its destruction. The 17th lost 37th BS B-26F-1 42-96305B/N 40 *Yehudi*, flown by 1Lt Valentine W Krug, during the first mission when its left engine was hit by flak over La Spezia. The pilot was unable to feather the propeller, and the Marauder quickly lost altitude and eventually made a good water landing off Corsica. The crew was rescued within five minutes by a British motor torpedo boat.

That same day, the 320th BG generated two missions to the Casalmaggiore railway bridge and the 319th BG attacked the Cremona road and railway bridge both in the morning and afternoon. The latter group's first mission scored no hits, as the target was obscured by smoke. The afternoon mission was the 319th's 300th, and when the B-26 crews found the target area clear of smoke, they successfully hit the bridge and its approaches. Flight Commander Col Holzapple saw a span dropping, but ordered a return the next day to make sure the target was destroyed.

The 319th's policy was now to revisit a target repeatedly until the bridge was totally destroyed. This tactic would make repairs almost impossible, and reduce losses by not allowing the enemy enough time to relocate effective flak defences to defend a damaged target.

More *Major Mallory* missions were flown by the wing on 13 July, with the 319th BG targeting a permanent pontoon bridge at Viedano. The Marauders destroyed an 1100-ft section of the bridge during another successful mission. The operation came to a close when all three groups returned to Piacenza on the 14th. Cloud interfered with some of the missions, and probable hits were again achieved, but the target would require more bombs to ensure its destruction.

B-26C-10 41-34883 B/N 38 *Jeanie* of the 37th BS/17th BG flies over Italy in formation with B-26G-5 43-34254 B/N 49 in the autumn of 1944 (*Bruce Kwiatkowski*)

A pilot's eye view from the cockpit of a B-26. The bomber to the left of the photograph is B-26B-30 41-31969 B/N 96 *Ruth Marie* of the 440th BS/319th BG. Visible in front of the pilot is the sighting ring used to aim the four fixed forward-firing package guns mounted in pairs on the fuselage sides. Originally designed for ground strafing, these guns were very occasionally fired by pilots at enemy fighters making head-on attacks. In practice the package guns were rarely used, and some – or all – of them were often removed by the MTO units to save weight (*Louise Hertenstein*)

The second half of July saw the wing attack nothing but Italian bridges. The targets were now more often further a field or, like Piacenza, needed to be revisited. The 319th BG flew a successful mission against the Denenzano railway viaduct on 15 July, when it dropped two spans at the eastern end of the structure with direct hits. The next day, the group sent out two 24-aircraft missions against the Piacenza bridge, and at least two spans were destroyed. On 19 July, the 319th hit the Ostiglia railway bridge for the first time, scoring possible hits.

Ostiglia was one of the few bridges left standing by this stage in the conflict, and, unusually, it was still defended by flak. Col Holzapple requested careful bombing so that the target would not need to be revisited. However, the results were not good enough, so the next day the 319th returned, along with the 17th BG. Both groups scored possible hits, but only half the bombs landed in the target area. This time the flak was heavy and accurate, and wrought havoc with the 319th BG.

Some 14 of the group's 23 Marauders were hit by flak, and B-26C-45 42-107554 of the 438th BS, flown by 1Lt George Marple, came down near the target. Two 440th BS bombers collided near Corsica, and B-26B-45 42-95793 B/N 85, flown by 1Lt Clifton Collins, crashed. Three crewmen parachuted from the bomber before it hit the ground.

The 17th BG also sustained a loss when B-26B-50 42-96021 B/N 22, flown by 1Lt J M Baker of the 34th BS, was hit in the left engine by flak as it left the target area. The bomber stalled and went into a spin, before crashing into the side of a mountain. Only two parachutes were seen. Amongst the crewmen lost was group CO Col Donald L Gilbert, who was flying his 94th mission at the time – the most completed by a 17th BG crewman up to that time. The two survivors were SSgts W B Donovan, who became a PoW, and William Russell, who evaded capture and later returned to his unit.

DRAGOON

Operation *Dragoo*n was the code name for the Allied invasion of southern France, which commenced on 15 August. Phase I of the operation (Operation *Uppercut*) began on 1 August, and the Marauder groups were assigned the task of destroying bridges that could be used by the Germans to send reinforcements to the invasion area. They were also

On 5 September for example, the 320th BG targeted a road bridge southeast of Pavia. The 443rd BS's lead B-26B-50 42-95937 B/N 84 was hit by flak over Forrobetti, and it dropped out of formation with its left propeller feathered. Four parachutes were seen as the Marauder headed north, losing altitude. Pilot Capt Luther Moyer, co-pilot 2Lt R H Nealy and gunner TSgt George Rolfe were captured, but radio operator/gunner Sgt Leonard Hoyne evaded and returned to his unit.

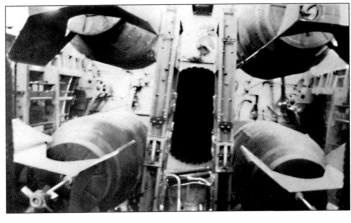

Looking forward in the Marauder towards the bulkhead behind the radio room, four 1000-lb bombs can be seen firmly held in place within the bomb-bay by their shackles. The normal bombload for a B-26 was 4000 lb. Alternatively, two 2000-lb bombs could be carried, or a higher number of smaller weapons such as parafrags or incendiary bombs (*Louise Hertenstein*)

Many of the Marauders were now racking up impressive mission tallies on their noses, including B-26C-45 42-107550 B/N 08 *O'Riley's Daughter* of the 319th BG/437th BS. The bomber passed the 100-mission mark (using its original engines) on 11 September when it was part of a formation that attacked defensive positions south of Santa Lucia.

That same day, Gen Mark Clark's Fifth Army launched a massive assault on the 'Gothic Line'. Again, the 42nd BW played an important role in the offensive by supporting US troops on the ground, its units targeting German forces in Casetta, Firenzuola, Florence, Mt Oggioli, Rimini, Pontecurone, Santa Lucia and Traversa over the next five days.

The 17th, 319th and 320th BGs flew multiple missions against defensive positions in the Firenzuola area on 12 September, although some targets were obscured by cloud. The two missions flown by the 319th BG, however, were particularly successful, with all but two bombs falling in the target area on the first mission, and the second inflicting yet more damage on the target. The wing would subsequently learn later that a German parachute regiment was wiped out during these raids.

The 17th BG's 37th BS suffered the day's only casualty when B-26G-5 43-34393 B/N 39, flown by 2Lt Thomas Hughes, crashed near Bologna. On the 13th, the wing targeted the rail system too, with the 319th BG rendering the Pontecurone rail bridge unusable by hitting the embankment above it – the resulting landslide blocked the track.

Missions continued to be flown from Sardinia whilst preparations were made for the 42nd BW's final base move in the MTO.

Capt Sidney 'Snuffy' Smith, who was CO of the 320th BG's 441st BS from 27 July 1944 through to 12 March 1945, sits in the cockpit of B-26B-50 42-96016 B/N 04 *Doris K./ lidalizeya*. This aeroplane was named for Smith's wife, Doris King Smith, and was adorned with her picture. The bomber is also the subject of the cover artwork, when it was flown by 1Lt Charles O'Mahony on the mission to Rovereto on 5 November 1944 (*via Franz Reisdorf*)

CORSICA

As the Allies pushed further into Italy, the 42nd BW found itself needing to move closer to its targets so to be able to offer better support to troops on the ground as they slowly advanced through the mountains in the country's northern regions. The recently liberated French island of Corsica was selected as the ideal location for the

B-26B-15 41-31590 B/N 79
REPULSIVE RABBIT of the 440th BS/
319th BG flew its 100th mission on
5 September 1944, and went on
to complete 125 missions with the
group. The bomber had previously
been named *Laura* and carried B/N
74 on its tail. *REPULSIVE RABBIT*
artwork appeared on both sides
of the B-26's nose, with slight
differences between the two
versions. The name only appeared
on the starboard side, however
(*Louise Hertenstein*)

Right
B-26C-15 41-34932 B/N 38
JOSEPHINE II of the 438th BS/319th
BG dives away to port after
dropping its bombs on an Italian
target in the Po Valley during late
1944. It was a standard defensive
manoeuvre employed by B-26 units
to dive away from a target to avoid
flak. The dive could be quite gentle,
or made at a G-inducing 45-degree
angle, depending on the intensity
and accuracy of the flak. *JOSEPHINE
II* was one of fifteen 319th BG
Marauders to fly more than 100
missions (*Louise Hertenstein*)

wing's three B-26 groups, and they commenced operations from their new bases on 22 September.

The 17th BG was now stationed at Poretta, the 319th BG at Serragia and the 320th BG at Alto. Following this change of base, the latter two groups had to revert to single-ship take-offs due to the airfield's narrower pierced-steel planking runways. The tighter confines of Serragia, in particular, provided the crews with some challenging moments. Indeed, on the 319th's first mission, several B-26s clipped trees at the end of the runway.

The first suggestion to counteract the problem was to reduce bomb loads from 4000 lb to 3000 lb until engineers had time to remove the trees. The wing, however, ordered the removal of the nose and waist guns (and their gunners) in an effort to lighten the group's B-26s. As the Luftwaffe was no longer making attacks, it appeared that at least some of the defensive armament was unnecessary.

On 23 September, the 319th BG's 439th BS suffered two losses when it attacked the Vigevano railway bridge. B-26B-50 42-95997 B/N 58 blew a tyre and crashed on take-off, but none of the crew was injured. B-26C-45 42-107555 B/N 58, flown by 1Lt Earl Peterson, was hit by flak over the target and went down – only four parachutes were seen.

All three groups were aloft on the 26th when they attacked a recently completed temporary road bridge at Ostiglia. Crews found the target to be heavily defended, and the 17th BG lost three Marauders to flak. B-26C-45 42-107535 B/N 28 *Shack Date*, flown by 1Lt Jacob Miller of the 37th BS, was abandoned by its crew, one of whom was group CO, Col R O Harrell, who returned to Corsica the next day. The remaining two Marauders (B-26G-5 43-34241 B/N 55 and B-26C-15 41-34921 B/N 63 *Helen*, both from the 95th BS) crash-landed at Borgo.

The 319th BG lost B-26B-45 42-95785 B/N 95 *Little Sue*, flown by Capt James L Bruson of the 440th BS, which was brought down by flak just after releasing its bombs. Finally, the 320th BG had five men injured when 24 of its 26 Marauders were hit by flak over the target.

The 319th BG flew to an unusual target on 30 September when its bombers attacked an underwater bridge at San Nazaro, near Rovereto. The target itself demonstrated the enemy's ingenuity in creating a temporary crossing that sat just under the surface of the water, and was therefore more difficult to spot from the air.

Although underwater bridges were sometimes difficult to locate, and hit, repeated air attacks usually destroyed them. And the Allies would return to cause yet more damage whenever they were repaired. Unfortunately for the Germans, the bridge at San Nazaro was visible from the air, and the 319th BG duly attacked it with 18 Marauders. The bridge, and the results of the mission, were not readily discernable to Photographic Intelligence personnel in the aftermath of the raid, however, and they reported that there were hits to the northern end and northern approaches of the 'probable bridge'.

As well as the usual targets of road and railway bridges, the groups also bombed fuel storage depots in late September and early October. On the first day of the latter month, the 17th BG flew three successful missions to the Erba fuel dump. A good concentration of bombs caused vast fires, and crews witnessed a smoke cloud rising to 7000 ft.

1 October also saw Col Holzapple announce that the 319th BG would be the first of the wing's groups to convert to the B-25 Mitchell. This news was received with a chorus of groans, as crews had hoped to receive A-26 Invaders instead. Production of the brand new bomber was running well behind schedule, however, so the wing had little choice but to switch to the B-26's arch rival instead, as Marauder production was now being scaled back.

319th BG personnel were now also aware that the group was far more likely to have to continue fighting in the Far East when Germany had finally been defeated. Fears of a delayed return home would ultimately prove to be correct, as the 319th flew against the Japanese in, ironically, A-26 Invaders between July and September 1945.

In the meantime, the group received new B-25s throughout October, allowing it to commence pilot conversion onto the type. Despite early misgivings, crews came to believe that the B-25 was as good as, if not better than, the B-26 in all respects bar one – it did not feel quite so safe over the target. The big advantage that the B-25 had over the B-26 was that it was a simpler aeroplane to maintain. The more complex Marauder needed a lot more attention from groundcrews in order to attain a good level of serviceability. These differences were also reflected in the unit cost of each type. In late 1944, the price tag for a B-26 was $192,427, whereas the B-25 cost only $116,752. By comparison, the unit cost of a B-17 was $187,742.

On 11 October MATAF and MASAF (Mediterranean Allied Strategic Air Force) launched Operation *Pancake* in support of the Fifth Army's advance in the Bologna area. Its aim was to destroy German supply routes, attack enemy troops and isolate the battle

Above
B-26C-45 42-107550 B/N 08
O'RILEY'S DAUGHTER of the 437th BS/319th BG was one of the many Marauders initially flown by the group in natural metal finish to be hastily painted in field-applied camouflage after March 1944. 42-107550 completed 110 missions with the 319th BG prior to being transferred to the 320th BG. By war's end, the bomber's mission tally stood at 165. This photograph was taken after the B-26 had joined the 320th BG, the names of its old crew and the 437th BS emblem that adorned its nose having been hastily painted out (*via Franz Reisdorf*)

B-26C-10 41-34895 B/N 76 *Twin Engine Queenie (II)* of the 439th BS/ 319th BG was also a mission centurion with the group prior to being transferred to the 95th BS/ 17th BG (*Louise Hertenstein*)

Photographed just after its retirement from the 319th BG, B-26C-45 42-107800 *LU LU* was assigned to the 438th BS, but at present its battle number remains unknown. Note the B-25 with B/N 26 applied to its cobalt blue tail fin in the background – Mitchells replaced Marauders in 319th BG service in October 1944. *LU LU* had 67 missions to its credit when it was transferred to the 444th BS/320th BG on 1 November 1944. Renamed *Judy*, the bomber was assigned B/N 89 (*Ronald Macklin*)

area, thus allowing US forces to breakthrough to the city. The Marauders would be tasked with hitting fuel dumps, munitions factories and depots, as well as the obligatory road and railway bridges.

On the first day of the offensive, the 319th BG flew its 399th and 400th missions when it attacked the Cassalecchio road bridge and the San Rufillo road/railway bridge – it missed both targets, however. Twenty-four B-26s from the group returned two days later, but only five crews could see to drop on their targets, claiming possible hits. Another five attacked the road bridge at Borgo Panigale, but missed. Six others hit yet another target of opportunity when they bombed the railway bridge north of Bologna.

On 19 October, Axis fighters attacked the Marauders for the first time in many months when the 319th and 320th BGs targeted the railway bridge at Mantua. Eighteen B-26s from the latter group attacked first, and suffered no losses. A dozen fighters then bounced 12 bombers from the 319th BG, the Bf 109s from the Italian co-belligerent air force (*Republica Sociale Italiana*) initially approaching from head on. They then got in behind the bombers and made attack runs to within 100 ft.

The B-26s had reduced defences, as both nose and waist guns had been removed. The crews made desperate radio calls to Allied fighters in the area, but received no response. The last flight was hit hard, and three 440th BS aeroplanes were downed – B-26C-45 42-107565 B/N 88 *Rodger the Dodger II*, flown by 1Lt Donald Treadwell, B-26C-45 42-107561 B/N 97 *Tally Ho*, flown by 1Lt John L O'Bryant, and B-26C-20 41-35041 B/N 93, flown by 2Lt Floyd W Roberts.

This devastating attack caused the 319th BG to abort its mission during the bomb run, but the 320th BG pressed on and destroyed the bridge. Amongst the group's aircraft taking part in this operation was veteran 441st BS B-26B-45 42-95753 B/N 08 *My Gal*, which flew its 100th mission on the 19th.

The 319th BG suffered yet another loss the next day when it targeted the Nevesa railway bridge and causeway. Two formations went for the bridge, while two other flights attacked nearby flak emplacements. The group gained possible hits on the causeway, and B-26C-45 42-107731 B/N 56, flown by 2Lt Dean Rice of the 439th BS, sustained a direct hit and exploded over the target.

The end of October saw the cancellation of many missions due to bad weather. After nine straight days of no flying, the 319th BG flew its final missions with the B-26 on the very last day of the month. Unfortunately, both 18-ship flights to the Piazzola and Montebello railway bridges missed their targets. Having been declared operational on the B-25 on 1 November, the group would return to both targets three days later.

By then the 319th's surplus B-26s had been sent to Naples for reconditioning, after which they were reassigned to other groups, including the 17th and 320th. Some personnel from the group were also transferred to other Marauder units in the 42nd BW, including Lt Col Ashley B Woolridge. He took command of the 320th BG on 3 November, having already flown 88 missions with the 319th BG.

Both the 17th and 320th BGs began November with a series of raids designed to stop the flow of supplies to German forces east of Lake Garda. On the 5th, eight Bf 109s, two Fw 190s and a pair of C.202s attacked 18 Marauders from the 320th BG heading for the Rovereto railway bridge. Before reaching the target, B-26G-5 43-34396 B/N 01, flown by 2Lt Truman C Cole, slid out of formation as the pilot fought to control the bomber. Three parachutes were seen before a wing came off and the aeroplane turned on its back, crashing into a mountain and exploding.

B-26C-45 42-107532 B/N 86, flown by 1Lt James N Logsdon was hit by flak as the group departed the target area. Dropping out of formation, the bomber's wheels came down and its nose briefly rose, before the Marauder spun down and hit the ground – again, only three parachutes were seen.

B-26G-5 43-34261 B/N 84, flown by 1Lt Charles W P Kaminski, was hit on its bomb run, but the crew still managed to get its ordnance away on target. When the bomb-bay doors opened, a great spray of fuel emerged, covering the rear of the aeroplane. Returning from the target, the bomber left the formation with a feathered engine, escorted by three B-26s. Kaminski tried to lower the landing gear, as he had no intention of bellying in with a bomb-bay full of fuel. However, the nose gear refused to lock down, so the crew baled out. Last to leave was Kaminski, who took to his parachute just as the bomber went into a spin. Air-sea rescue picked up the crew.

Despite the flak and fighters, the 320th had still managed to hit the target with a good concentration of bombs.

On 6 November Operation *Bingo* was launched by the 42nd BW, with the aim of stopping supplies coming into northern Italy from Austria and Yugoslavia via the Brenner Pass. That day, the wing targeted the Innsbruck-Verona electric railway line, with both groups flying three missions apiece. The Marauders then switched their focus to helping a new British Eighth Army offensive, with two missions being flown against troop concentrations at Forli on the 7th.

The following day, B-26s from the 320th BG attempted to hit the Sant'Anastasio railway bridge but missed, scoring hits on the southern approach instead. Breaking away from the target, B-26C-45 42-107556 had an engine knocked out by flak. The bomber, flown by the 444th BS operations officer Capt David Hammond Jr, spun in, killing all on board.

On 16 November, 18 B-26s from the 320th BG tried to bomb the Santa Margherita railway bridge, but again they missed their target. Nevertheless, the line was severed by ordnance that landed just north of the tracks. Flak was encountered 30 seconds before bomb release, and it continued until the Marauders broke away over Rovereto. Ten aircraft were damaged, and veteran B-26B-10 41-18190 B/N 89, flown by 1Lt Russel W Jones of the 444th BS, dropped out of the formation when it lost an engine to flak. It was last seen at 4500 ft being escorted by P-47s.

Three days later, the 320th BG attacked the railway bridge at Sant'Ambrogio di Valpolicella, whilst the 17th BG targeted the railway bridge at San Michele. As bombers from the latter group were breaking away from the target, intense flak downed 95th BS B-26G-5 43-34398 B/N 52, flown by 1Lt Ollie B Childs.

On 20 November, the groups attacked the Rovereto railway bridge once again, but this time no losses were sustained. These were the last missions flown by B-26s over Italy, bringing to an end the Marauder's participation in the war in MTO.

The 42nd BW had initially planned to move both groups from Corsica to bases on the Italian mainland so as to be closer to the action, but the move was shelved when the airfields that had been selected were deemed to be unsuitable for B-26 operations. Both groups would head to France instead, thus consolidating all B-26s units in the ETO. However, the 17th and 320th BGs would form part of the Franco-American First Tactical Air Force (Provisional), rather than being assigned to the Ninth Air Force, which controlled the remaining USAAF Marauder groups then in-theatre.

B-26C-45 42-107617 B/N 80 *Dizzy Blond* of the 432nd BS/17th BG was yet another centenarian, and the bomber is seen here with 115 missions to its credit. The port engine bears the name *Sylvia* – it was common practice for groundcrews to name the engine for which they were responsible. The pair of 1850 hp Pratt & Whitney R-2800-39 Double Wasp air-cooled radials drove four-bladed 13 ft 6 in diameter Curtiss Electric propellers, which are seen here in the X position. This was a safety measure to help prevent damage in the event of gear failure whilst on the ground (*Alf Egil Johannessen*)

ETO OFFENSIVE

In late November 1944, the 17th and 320th BGs moved to Longvic, near the city of Dijon, in eastern France. Now just 75 miles from Germany, the 42nd BW was assigned to the 1st Tactical Air Force (Provisional) to provide air support for the Sixth Army Group.

On 1 December the 17th BG flew its first mission from its new base to Breisach railway bridge, but cloud cover forced crews to bomb Kaiserslautern barracks instead. The 320th BG enjoyed more success when it bombed Rastatt railway bridge later that day, cutting the line south of the structure. The group went back to Rastatt on the 5th and the 10th, only to be thwarted by cloud on both occasions. The winter of 1944-45 produced some of the worst weather seen in western Europe in 50 years, hampering operations in December and January. There would be many recalls, and obscured and missed targets during this period.

On 13, 14 and 17 December, the 17th BG hit defensive positions within the 'Siegfried Line'. On the latter date, its crews undertook two missions to the Ober-Otterbach area, and flak claimed 37th BS B-26B-40 42-43278 B/N 36 *JERSEY BOUNCER III*, flown by 1Lt Donald V Leslie. This veteran Marauder had served with the group since 12 September 1943, and was on its 130th mission. 34th BS B-26B-40 42-43312 *Wolves' Delight*, flown by 1Lt Wayne J Hutchinson, was also heavily damaged by flak, and its crew baled out once back over Allied territory.

The 320th BG hit the 'Siegfried Line' on the 14th and 17th, and the accuracy of the bombing during the second raid earned the two formation leaders DFCs.

On 19 December, the 17th BG targeted bridges at Neckargemünd. B-26G-5 43-34238 B/N 73 *Erma*, flown by 2Lt Lane E Spence of the 95th BS, was shot down by Bf 109s as it approached the target. That same day, the 320th BG tried to hit the Neustadt railway marshalling yards through cloud cover and missed the target by half-a-mile.

On the 23rd it was the 320th BG's turn to hit the Breisach bridge. During the course of the operation, veteran 441st BS B-26B-45 42-95753 B/N 08 *My Gal*, flown by 2Lt Richard E Dickey, suffered a direct flak hit in the bomb-bay and broke in two whilst flying its 115th mission. There were no survivors.

Christmas Eve saw Bf 109s claim three more Marauders from the 17th BG as they headed for the Messerschmitt aircraft factory at Frederickshafen. Having missed the rendezvous with their fighter escorts, the bomber crews carried on alone, and were attacked before they commenced their bomb run. All assigned to the 37th BS, the three aircraft that went down were B-26B-50 42-96003 B/N 45 *Ramblin'*

The weather on mainland Europe during the winter of 1944-45 was some of the worst ever recorded during the 20th century. Heavy cloud cover caused the cancellation of missions due to Dijon being declared unsafe for operations or targets being obscured by thick overcast. Here, 17th BG Marauders in the group's dispersal area have had their noses and cockpits covered with tarpaulins to prevent icing and a build up of snow. Groundcrews worked hard to keep the B-26s operational during this period, with the removal of snow from the flight surfaces being a particularly onerous task. The veteran Marauder in the foreground has lost almost all the camouflage paint that was once applied to its engine cowlings. The second bomber in the line up is a former 319th BG machine, with a field-applied camouflage scheme. The straight demarcation line between the bomber's olive drab uppersurfaces and natural metal undersides contrasts with the factory-applied scheme worn by the B-26 closest to the camera. The latter has a wavy demarcation line between the uppersurface camouflage and neutral grey undersides
(*Bruce Kwiatkowski*)

B-26G-1 43-34192 B/N 38 *Suzy Mae* of the 442nd BS/320th BG was a former Ninth Air Force Marauder that was transferred to the group in late 1944. Jack J Haher, 444th BS/320th BG pilot, gave his views on the flight characteristics of the later model Marauder. 'My first recollection of the G-model was at Barksdale. I picked one up at Hunter Army Air Base to deliver to the French at Tunis. I would say good riddance, and it couldn't happen to a better bunch of folks! The main reason for this comment was speed – the B-26G was slow! Also, the wing's higher incidence of attack made its flight appearance look "funny/ugly". The aircraft's wings and engines look like they were going uphill by themselves, and nothing else was following!' (*via Franz Reisdorf*)

Wreck, flown by 2Lt Alvin W Chadoir, and B-26C-45s 42-107563 B/N 42 *Teton Special*, flown by 2Lt Fred E Bulleit, and 42-107768 B/N 35 *This Is It II*, flown by 1Lt Fred W Abbott. The crews of *Teton Special* and *This Is It II* all took to their parachutes and were subsequently captured, but only gunner Sgt Hayslip escaped from *Ramblin' Wreck* to become a PoW.

By contrast, on the same day the 320th BG suffered no losses when it bombed the Langenargen railway bridge. Lead navigator 1Lt Bernard C Delosier aboard B-26C-45 42-107752 B/N 88 *Miss Arkansas* was awarded the DFC for guiding the formation past defences and destroying the target. Twenty-four hours later, 320th BG lead bombardier Capt Charles M Traynor Jr was also awarded the DFC for bombing accuracy against the Singen bridge. During the same mission, a formation from the 444th BS dropped its bombs on neutral Switzerland. An inquiry into the matter subsequently deemed that the crews had made an honest mistake.

On 26 December the 320th BG again missed the Rastatt Bridge, and the next day it went back to the Kaiserslautern barracks. Cloud thwarted crews, so they dropped on the nearby Oos barracks instead. The 17th BG flew three more missions to the Kaiserslautern barracks on 29 and 30 December and 1 January 1945. On the last of these operations (undertaken with the 320th BG), flak claimed lead B-26B-40 42-43308 B/N 68 *NEW YORK CENTRAL II*, flown by 1Lt Joseph T Shoeps, with 95th BS CO Maj Hugh H Teitsworth also on board.

The 2nd saw the 320th BG hit gun positions at Nunschwiller and a supply depot at Oos, whilst the 17th BG targeted Thaleischweiler barracks. The weather then grounded the B-26s until 16 January, when the 320th BG bombed the Rastatt bridge again. Leading the attack was B-26C-45 42-107778 B/N 70 *The Termite* of the 443rd BS, which was flying its 300th mission. That same day the 17th BG hit the Campe de Bitche barracks in northern France. The 34th BS lost its CO, Capt James A King Jr, during the mission when B-26C-45 42-107725 B/N 11, flown by Capt D D Bartels, was hit by flak and crashed. Flak also claimed B-26G-5 43-34251 B/N 04, flown by 1Lt H F Reed of the 34th BS.

On 19 January the 17th BG also targeted the Rastatt bridge, but its crews failed to find it. B-26B-50 42-95892 B/N 68 crashed on its return to Longvic. The 320th BG went after the Achern railway marshalling yards that same day, but it too struggled to find its target due to thick cloud. The formation attacked the alternate target at Lahr instead.

B-26G-11 43-34605 *My Gall II* B/N 08, flown by 2Lt Arthur L McCurdy of the 441st BS, left the formation with engine trouble. The aeroplane was on its very first mission, having been brought in as a replacement for *My Gal*, which had been lost over Breisach bridge on 23 December. The last report received from the crew was that they were going to bale out five miles from Besancon, in France. McCurdy, however, attempted to land on one engine, but the B-26 cartwheeled when it touched down and its bombs exploded, killing the entire crew.

The 17th BG again failed to find the Rastatt bridge on 22 January, and this time B-26C-45 42-107724 *Janette* crashed after take-off and B-26C-45 42-107792 B/N 77, flown by 1Lt Jack E McKenzie of the 432nd BS, lost an engine to flak and crashed en route to the target.

On 2 February the 320th BG bombed ammunition and fuel dumps at Ransbach and Zell, respectively, whilst the 17th targeted the Offenburg barracks. Six days later the latter group revisited the Rastatt bridge, whilst the 320th BG sent bombers to attack the Loffingen and Hornberg bridges and Lahr barracks. Lt Col Woolridge led the 320th BG

back to the bridges the next day, and although they were partially obscured by clouds, a possible hit was observed.

At the very start of what would prove to be yet another weather-blighted mission – to Labach railway marshalling yards – on 13 February, B-26B-40 42-43302 B/N 25 *Row'n Home* (a veteran of 135 missions) of the 442nd BS/320th BG crashed on take-off. Its pilots, 1Lt Sylvester W LaChasse and Maj Paul S Jordan, were both seriously injured. The following day, the 320th BG finally managed to bomb the Labach yards, destroying rolling stock and ammunition depots. The explosions caused smoke plumes that could be seen 35 miles away, topping out at 10,000 ft.

On the 15th, the 17th BG struck gun positions at St Ingeberge, on the 'Siegfried Line', and the following day it bombed the Lauterbad railway bridge, whilst the 320th BG targeted the Offenburg railway marshalling yards. On 19 February it hit barracks and supply areas at Lahr. That same day the 17th BG targeted the Nahe river railway bridge at Bad Munster, and it joined forces with the 320th to finish it off three days later.

The 42nd BW supported Operation *Clarion* from 22 February, the aim of this campaign being to neutralise the enemy's badly damaged transport system. The 17th and 320th BGs hit railway marshalling yards at Uberlingen, Meeskirch and Ludwigshafen on this date, and bombed the railway bridge at Standenbuhl the following day. On the 24th, the railway marshalling yards at Neustadt were attacked, and both groups struck the bomb dump at Siegelsbach on 25 February and 1 March.

During the latter mission, the 320th BG was unable to drop its bombs due to cloud, and the 17th BG had two aircraft crash upon their return to base – B-26G-11 43-34607 B/N 63 and veteran B-26C-20 41-35014 B/N 62 *Lil Angel's Big Sis*. The 17th BG returned to Siegelsbach on 2 March, while 45 B-26s of the 320th BG bombed the

B-26B-40-MA B/N 68 42-43308 *NEW YORK CENTRAL II* **of the 95th BS/ 17th BG was paid for by the employees of the New York Central Railroad. Its predecessor, B-26B-2 41-17916** *NEW YORK CENTRAL***, was paid for by the same company, and it was destroyed in a crash-landing on 24 February 1943.** *New York Central II* **flew over 100 missions before being downed by flak on 1 January 1945 (***Bruce Kwiatkowski***)**

B-26C-45 42-107724 B/N 83 *Janette* **of the 432nd BS/17th BG was regularly flown by 1Lt John G Fabian's crew. The aeroplane was destroyed when it crashed shortly after take-off during the group's second abortive mission to the Rastatt Bridge on 22 January 1945. The port engine was ripped off its mounts during the belly landing, and further damage was caused by the rescue crews working to free the pilot and co-pilot. The aeroplane's name was written on both sides of its nose in red (***Bruce Kwiatkowski***)**

Top, above and below
B-26B-40 42-43302 B/N 25 *Row'n Home* was named and flown by 1Lt 'Big John' Rowan of the 442nd BS/ 320th BG. The aeroplane crashed on take-off at the start of its 136th mission on 13 February 1945, seriously injuring its pilots, 1Lt Sylvester W LaChasse and Maj Paul S Jordan (*via Franz Reisdorf*)

Haslach railway marshalling yards. The 17th BG went to the ammunition dump at Neuenkirchen on the 3rd, whilst the 320th BG attempted to bomb a similar target at Kirkel, but was again thwarted by cloud.

SHORAN

On 10 March, 320th BG Deputy Group CO Lt Col Larry Hayward, flying in the only Short Range Air Navigation (SHORAN) equipped Marauder then available – B-26G-10 43-34463 B/N 45 of the 17th BG – led his group on its first Blind Approach Technique (BAT) bombing mission against the Hauenstein supply depot, which was covered by cloud. Three days later the 17th BG used the technique for the first time to bomb Bad Kreuznach, which was again obscured by solid cloud.

The driving force behind SHORAN was RCA Industry Service Laboratory scientist Stuart Seeley, who, in 1937, had been given the task of eliminating 'ghosts' from television screens. These duplicate images are the result of reflected transmitter signals from buildings or other objects arriving at the receiver a fraction of a second later than the direct signal, thereby causing overlapping images on a TV screen.

During his experiments, Seeley deduced that the distance between the main image and the ghost on the screen could provide a means for measuring the extra distance travelled by the secondary image. If the position of the transmitter was known precisely, the distance measurement could indicate the source of the reflection. This phenomenon could, therefore, form the basis of an accurate system for measuring distances. Thus, SHORAN was born.

When equipped with SHORAN, an aeroplane could determine its precise position in any weather, day or night, by sending a signal to a pair of ground transmitters at known locations that reflected the signal back to its source. Seeley's new system was first tested in a B-17 in August 1942, and the results achieved were amazing. SHORAN could, however, only be used against stationary targets, and it had a maximum range of 300 statute miles. It also needed a clear radio path (line of sight), which meant that the SHORAN-equipped bomber had to fly at an altitude of at least 14,000 ft, depending on the location of the ground sets.

The first combat mission using this technology was conducted on the night of 10 December 1944 when 57th BW B-25s operating from Corsica destroyed the Fidenza railway bridge near Bologna. Both the 17th and 320th BGs began training with the new system in late 1944, and they dropped their first practice bombs on 7 February 1945.

When the two groups employed the system operationally, it would sometimes give a bombing accuracy of 99 per cent. SHORAN also proved its worth against targets such as troop concentrations that were indistinct to even the legendary Norden bombsight.

A lead ship equipped with SHORAN would be the guide for the other B-26s to drop their bombs – this was also the standard tactic used by a Norden-equipped lead ship. And because there were only a handful of SHORAN-equipped B-26s in the ETO, it soon became common practice for a Marauder from one unit to lead another squadron to its target. For example, on 11 March, 444th BS SHORAN B-26 B/N 87, flown by 1Lt Jackson W Brainerd of the 443rd BS, led the 320th BG in an attack on the Bad Münster railway bridge. The next day 443rd BS B-26G-5 43-34255 B/N 29, flown by 1Lt Elmer H Schrantz of the 441st, did the same against the ammunition dump at Kirkel-Neuhäusel.

On 13 March, 57 B-26s from the 320th BG attacked the ammunition dump and supply areas at Kirkel-Neuhäusel, and on the 14th the group dropped the Bad Munster railway bridge. Between 15 and 18 March, both groups supported Operation *Undertone* – the Seventh Army's breakthrough of the 'Siegfried Line' near Zweibrucken.

During the mission on the 15th, Brig Gen John P Doyle, commander of the 42nd BW, led the 320th BG in 441st BS B-26G-5 43-34257 B/N 10, with Lt Col Larry Hayward as his co-pilot. Upon the completion of this sortie, the latter became the first Marauder crewman to fly 100 missions in a tour – all with the 320th BG. The bomber was promptly named *Clearfield* after Hayward's home town. He flew his 101st mission that afternoon in 443rd BS B-26C-45 42-107778 B/N 70 *The Termite*.

The 320th BG was rewarded for its actions that day with a second DUC, as its accurate bombing had allowed Seventh Army to cross the 'Siegfried Line' virtually unopposed. On 18 March, the group bombed the Weidenthal railway bridge and the Neustadt-an-der-Weinstraße railway marshalling yards. The next day, the 320th flew its last mission against the 'Siegfried Line' when it hit defensive positions at Erlenbach.

The 320th attacked road/rail targets at Lambrecht and Hauenstein on the 20th. The following day, the groups hit the Eberstadt bomb dump, and on the 22nd the 320th targeted Heidelberg railway marshalling yards and a nearby bridge – lead ship B-26C-45 42-107785 B/N 27, flown by 1Lt Sylvester B Goeke, was downed by flak, taking with it the 442nd BS CO, Capt Carragher. He was replaced by Maj Deatley, CO of the 441st BS, and command of the latter was given to Capt Charles O'Mahony.

The 320th BG bombed Neckarelz railway bridge on 23 March, whilst the 17th BG returned to the Heidelberg railway marshalling yards once again. The group lost 34th BS B-26B-45 42-95786 B/N 20 *Skipper*, flown by 1Lt Arthur D Dudley, to intense flak – the crew baled out. The 17th BG also bombed the Kochendorf railway bridges near Heilbronn that same day, whilst the 320th targeted the Neckarelz railway bridge, but missed. On the 24th, the 320th BG attacked the Bietigheim-Bissingen railway viaduct before the weather halted all flying for a week. Both groups then hit the Heilbronn railway marshalling yards on 31 March.

In April, the 17th and 32oth BGs targeted enemy troops and supply depots, rather than what was left of the transportation system, which the Allies now needed left intact to help facilitate their rapid advance.

BAT MAN has nose art that reflects the fact that the aeroplane was fitted with SHORAN (Short Range Air Navigation) equipment, which was codenamed BAT (Blind Approach Technique). Although the full identity of this 17th BG Marauder remains unknown, it may well be the 37th BS's B-26G-10 43-34463 B/N 45, which was the 42nd BW's first SHORAN-equipped Marauder. On 10 March 1945, this aircraft led the 320th BG on its first BAT bombing mission against the Hauenstein supply depot, which was covered by cloud (*Bruce Kwiatkowski*)

On the 1st, the 320th BG flew a SHORAN mission to Vaihingen barracks and depot area. Not trained in BAT bombing, Capt Charles O'Mahony was the flight commander rather than the lead pilot on this mission, serving as co-pilot to 1Lt Elmer H Schrantz in 444th BS B-26 B/N 87. O'Mahony's navigator, 1Lt Joseph B Mirabella, in the nose of the aircraft announced that they were directly over the target, but the B-26's bombardier, 1Lt Samuel Liever, who was sat in the navigator's compartment using the SHORAN equipment, was convinced that they were yet to reach the target.

Moments later, O'Mahony looked back and saw the B-26 formation behind him dropping their bombs, so he ordered the aircraft's ordnance to be salvoed. The formation broke hard away from the target just as flak erupted in the very area they were supposed to have flown through. They would resolve what went wrong with the SHORAN guidance back at base, but for the time being they were thankful not to have been hit.

Two DFCs were awarded following this mission. 1Lt Lester D Wernick, who was lead navigator of the 443rd BS aboard B-26G-5 43-34255 B/N 29, got his for guiding the formation through the flak corridor to the target. 444th BS lead pilot Capt Cornelius A Trimm Jr was rewarded for continuing to guide his formation to the target despite his B-26C-45 (42-107846 B/N 83) having been badly damaged by flak.

On 2 April the 17th BG struck the Boblingen transport works, whilst the 320th BG bombed the Tübingen barracks and supply area. B-26 crews ended this mission at their new base at Dole, near Tavaux. Located 50 miles closer to the German border, it brought both groups nearer to their targets during the final weeks of the conflict in the ETO.

Between 5 and 9 April the 42nd BW bombed ammunition dumps at Kleinenstingen and Gailenkirchen. The following day, in direct support of the American 42nd Division's assault on Schweinfurt, both groups bombed the city's defences. The 17th BG was awarded its second DUC for its part in the operation. On 11 April the 320th BG targeted the Geislingen fuel dump and Bühl ammunition dump, returning to the same target the next day. On the 15th and 16th, both groups were called upon to hit the defences at Jaffé and Coubre, at the mouth of the Gironde River, where the Germans were still holding out against the French.

On 17 April, the 17th and 320th BGs bombed the Altendettelsau ammunition dump. Minutes later, the Marauders were attacked for the first time by Me 262 jet fighters. Six machines from JV 44, led by Generalleutnant Adolf Galland, made several passes at the bombers. The jet flown by Unteroffizier Eduard Schallmoser flew through the formation without firing its guns – they had jammed. The remaining five aircraft inflicted heavy damage on the B-26s with their deadly 30 mm cannon, however.

B-26C-10 41-34883 B/N 38 *Jeanie* of the 37th BS/17th BG is seen here at Dole, in France, after completing 84 missions and claiming two enemy fighters destroyed. It was retired shortly after this photograph was taken, having been declared war weary. Note that *Jeanie's* nose wheel bulge has been painted red. This was a late war unit marking adopted by all squadrons in the 17th BG, with red being the 37th BS's colour (*Bruce Kwiatkowski*)

34th BS tail gunner SSgt James A Valimont was seriously wounded by fire from an Me 262, yet he continued to man his guns in the shattered remnants of his tail position and claimed hits on another jet. Valimont was awarded a DFC for his actions. Fellow 17th BG gunner Sgt Chestnutt claimed an Me 262 shot down, and JV 44 did indeed lose a jet on this day. The German interceptors eventually broke off their attack when P-47 escorts arrived on the scene.

443rd BS B-26C-45 42-107753 B/N 58 *Peggy*, flown by 1Lt Edward F Joliff, landed at Sandhofen with an engine knocked out, and 441st BS B-26G-5 43-34389 B/N 03, flown by 2Lt Vernon O McGaffin, returned to Dole with a massive hole in its port wing. The next day, both groups retaliated by hitting the Luftwaffe landing grounds at Schussenried. Flak damaged B-26C-45 42-107531 B/N 21 *Lady Lynn* and wounded its pilot, 1Lt Walter E Barrett. Co-pilot 1Lt Paul Ramsey took control of the burning aeroplane and successfully crash-landed it at an airfield near Nancy. This proved to be the last 320th BG Marauder lost in combat. 443rd BS tail gunner SSgt Edgar A Beale aboard B-26B-45 42-95754 B/N 65 *Boomerang II* was killed by shrapnel during this mission.

On 19 and 20 April, the 320th BG hit Ingolstadt Kösching bomb dump, and one of its formations scored direct hits that saw flames reaching a height of 4000 ft during a series of secondary explosions.

Both groups bombed the Schwabmünchen ammunition dump on the 24th, and this time they were challenged by 11 jets from JV 44, led by high-scoring ace Oberst Günther Lützow. The 320th BG's decoy flight, headed up by 1Lt Billy Halbert in veteran B-26C-20 41-35031 B/N 66 *Old Faithful*, was attacked by two jets, one of which fired R4M rockets at the bombers. An Me 262 could carry up to 24 of these unguided weapons, and they were ripple fired from a range of 1000 yards or less. When salvoed en masse, the rockets formed a large field of fire that could not fail to hit a bomber formation. And a single rocket could down a bomber.

In this instance, the B-26 decoy flight was comprised of just three aircraft, and they suffered no damage. The 17th BG's main formation would not be so lucky. Two jets attacked from 'five o'clock', their R4Ms streaking through the formation and hitting B-26C-45 42-107729 B/N 17 *STUD DUCK*, piloted by 1Lt Fred J Harms of the 34th BS. The blast from an R4M blew engineer/gunner SSgt Edward F Truver out of his waist position, and he parachuted to safety. Truver landed near the burning wreck of 42-107729, which contained the remains of his crew. The 34th BS also lost B-26B-50 42-95987 B/N 20 *YO-YO CHAMP*, the Marauder having only transferred in from the 344th BG during March.

The 320th BG bombed the Ebenhausen munitions factory on the 25th, whilst the 17th BG returned to Schwabmünchen. The group's P-47 escort deterred attacks from German jet fighters, many of which were photographed on the ground by the B-26s at nearby Lechfeld – these were actually unserviceable aircraft that had been abandoned by fleeing Jagdwaffe units. The 42nd BW hastily mounted an all out attack on the airfield with fragmentation bombs the following day.

In response to the approaching Marauders, JV 44 scrambled 12 jets, again led by Generalleutnant Galland, from Innsbruck-Hötting. The Me 262s met the 17th BG B-26s almost head-on just as they started their bomb run. The jets passed over them at high speed without firing, then

B-26C-45 42-107729 B/N 17 *STUD DUCK* of the 34th BS/17th BG was shot down by Me 262s from JV 44 over Schwabmünchen on 24 April 1945. The only survivor from 1Lt Fred J Harms' crew that day was waist gunner SSgt Edward F Truver, who was blown out of the aircraft by the explosion caused by the R4M rocket that struck the bomber. *STUD DUCK* was assigned to Capt W D Lasly, whose name appeared beneath the pilot's window. As well as featuring 'Donald Duck' nose art, the B-26 also had its nose wheel cover adorned with a rendition of 'Mickey Mouse' (*Bruce Kwiatkowski*)

turned to attack from the 'eight o'clock' position. Unteroffizier Eduard Schallmoser, in Me 262A-1a 'White 14', fired his R4Ms into the formation and saw a B-26 blow up. As more jets attacked, more bombers went down.

Galland destroyed one B-26 and damaged another, before being hit by fire from TSgt Harry Dietz, who was a gunner in the lead 17th BG bomber flown by Maj Luther Gurkin. The escorting P-47s of the 50th FG then intervened, helping to stop further attacks. Thunderbolt pilot 1Lt James J Finnegan of the 10th FS hit Galland's already damaged Me 262A-1a with a two-second burst of fire, wounding the 104-kill ace and putting him out of action for the rest of the war.

Three Marauders went down over the target area, namely B-26F-1 42-96328 B/N 25, flown by 1Lt Kenneth L Bedor of the 37th BS, B-26G-20 44-68076 B/N 98 *Big Red*, flown by 1Lt Alf Shatto of the 432nd BS, and B-26B-40 42-43311 B/N 17 *Spot Cash*, flown by 1Lt Earl J Reeves Jr of the 34th BS. 37th BS B-26B-45 42-95771 *My Gal Sal*, flown by 1Lt Carl Johanson, also had an engine knocked out during the attacks, but the bomber made it back to the P-47 base at Luneville and crash-landed.

The 320th BG also flew three missions against Lechfeld that day, one of which was headed up by B-26C-45 42-107778 B/N 70 *The Termite*, with lead pilot Lt Col Lawrence J Hayward at the controls. None of the 320th BG formations could find the target due to cloud, however, and they returned unscathed with their bombs.

On 30 April and 1 May, both groups again attacked pockets of the Wehrmacht that continued to engage the Allies in northwest France, hitting minefields, gun positions and troop concentrations on the Île d'Oléron. The second of the eight missions flown by the 17th BG on 30 April took the group's overall tally past the 600 mark. A French amphibious force attacked the island later that day, and the B-26s used SHORAN to hit the enemy's defensive positions. The German garrison surrendered on the evening of the 1st.

The weather then intervened once again, ensuring that no more combat missions would be flown before the cessation of hostilities at midnight on 8 May 1945. With the war in Europe at an end, both groups relocated to different airfields in Germany, where some personnel engaged in disarmament work whilst others awaited orders to go home. The disarmament programme involved cataloguing and saving Luftwaffe material deemed to be of use, and destroying everything else.

All of the 42nd BW's assigned B-26s were either given to the French air force or, in most cases, flown to Landsberg and rendered useless by explosive charges. They were then summarily scrapped. Very few Marauders survived, and as if to help erase the memory of the aeroplane, the A-26 Invader was re-designated the B-26 post-war.

B-26B-50 42-95987 B/N 71-S *YO-YO CHAMP* flew more than 100 missions with the Ninth Air Force's 497th BS/344th BG. The aeroplane was named after its assigned pilot, 1Lt A J Wood, who was said to resemble the cartoon character 'Chicken Little'! Following its transfer to the 34th BS/17th BG as B/N 20 in late March 1945, *YO-YO CHAMP* enjoyed only a brief career with the 17th BG that lasted for less than a month. It was the group's second Marauder to be shot down over Schwabmünchen by Me 262s from JV 44 on 24 April 1945 (*Bruce Kwiatkowski*)

APPENDICES

B-26 CAMOUFLAGE AND MARKINGS

When the three B-26 groups first entered combat with the Twelfth Air Force, their aircraft wore no markings other than the national insignia and the radio call number on the fin. The latter was an abbreviated form of the bomber's serial number. For example, 41-17765 carried the number '117765' on its tail, and the aircraft was referred to simply as '765'. Many of the Marauders did, however, sport nose art prior to them reaching the MTO.

The first marking system to identify individual aircraft within a squadron was introduced by the 320th BG in early 1943, and it utilised white capital letters 20 to 24 inches in height applied to the rear fuselage. The group also applied the last three digits of the serial to the leading edge of the wing above and below the rubber de-icing boots. Early 320th aircraft B-26B-4 41-18017 *Devil's Playmate* also sported two red bands on a yellow-painted tail-cone. This marking may have been a short-lived attempt to distinguish a lead ship. Some early B-26s also sported the yellow surround applied to the early style national insignia that was used during Operation *Torch*.

As more B-26s became available, and all three groups operated in close proximity to each other, it became necessary to employ a marking system to distinguish each of the group aircraft. The first of these was introduced in July 1943, and it took the form of a ten-inch wide band applied to the tail (their exact size and location could vary) in group colours – red for the 17th BG, blue for the 319th BG and yellow for the 320th BG. These bands were often edged with white to help them stand out against the olive drab camouflage.

In October 1943 the 42nd BW introduced 48-inch 'battle numbers' to the fins of their aircraft, and these identified an individual B-26's squadron assignment and, later, its group assignment. The battle numbers replaced the radio call letters, but many older Marauders were seen with both markings applied. The battle numbers were initially painted white, with 1 to 24 assigned to the first squadron in each group, 25 to 49 for the next squadron, 50 to 74 for the third squadron and, finally, 75 to 99 for the last squadron.

Again, the exact size and location of the battle numbers varied, and the three groups positioned the numbers in their own individual ways. The 17th BG placed them high on the fin wholly over the radio call number, whilst the 319th BG applied its numbers usually below, but sometimes overlapping, the radio call number. The 320th BG also placed its numbers below the radio call number, using much thicker strokes.

Within a few weeks the battle numbers were re-applied in group colours, with the 17th BG edging its red numbers with white. When B-26s were delivered without camouflage, the edging was changed to black on both battle numbers and tail bands.

When the battle numbers were changed to the group colours, individual squadron colours began to be applied as well. The 17th BG also applied individual squadron colours to the propeller bosses of its aircraft too – blue for the 34th BS, red for the 37th BS, yellow for the 95th BS and white for

the 432nd BS. The group also applied the squadron colour to the nose wheel door bulge on many of its Marauders later in the war.

The 319th BG painted the forward cowl rings and the occasional propeller boss in squadron colours too – blue for the 437th BS, red for the 438th BS, yellow for the 439th BS and white for the 440th BS. The 320th BG applied red to the propeller bosses of all of its aircraft, and often to the cowl rings as well. The group's Marauders were almost always adorned with the appropriate squadron insignia on the forward fuselage too. The 319th BG's 437th BS was the only other squadron to apply its insignia in this way.

Some of the squadron insignia also evolved over time as well, with the 441st BS's emblem seeing three distinct design changes. The 443rd BS used a version of its 'running duck' on many of its aeroplanes, whilst the 444th BS initially had many of its B-26s adorned with the units 'rabbit' emblem. Later, the 444th BS applied a distinctive sharksmouth design to the majority of its bombers.

Nose art and names were painted onto B-26s from the start. It was the groundcrews that had the most association with an aeroplane, so it was usually the Marauder's crew chief that would bestow a name. It was rare for an aeroplane to be associated with a particular flight crew, as available crews usually flew whichever aircraft was serviceable. There were many exceptions, however. A senior pilot would sometimes be able to use a favourite B-26 for the majority of his missions, and he would occasionally get to name the aircraft too.

The camouflage worn by early B-26s in the MTO was the standard Olive Drab with Medium Gray undersides. Later B-models would have additional patches of Medium Green applied in various ways. This was formulated on B-26B-40 models, with scalloping to the wings, tail and fin. Camouflage was discontinued altogether on the B-26C-20, F- and G-models, with these aircraft being delivered in their natural metal finish.

During May 1944 there were a number of nocturnal intruder missions made on Decimomannu airfield, and a raid on a B-25 base on Corsica caused considerable damage. This prompted the 319th BG to conduct an experiment on the night of 15 May, when it dropped flares over the airfield to see how easily its B-26s could be spotted on the ground. The natural metal aircraft were all too visible, so from then on all the group's bombers had camouflage re-applied to their uppersurfaces. There is as yet no photographic evidence to prove that the other two B-26 groups followed suit, although a number of the 319th BG's Marauders with field-applied camouflage were later transferred to the 17th and 320th BGs when the 319th converted to Mitchells in November 1944.

Due to the increased risk of attacks on airfields in France, the USAAF ordered the re-introduction of camouflage to the uppersurfaces in the autumn of 1944. This was done in the field by all Marauder units, and many B-26Gs were painted before delivery with a standardised version of the Olive Drab scheme. Many aircraft, however, continued to conduct combat operations without the paint ever being applied.

COLOUR PLATES

1

B-26B-2-MA 41-17858 *COUGHIN' COFFIN* of the 34th BS/17th BG, Djedeida, Tunisia, October 1943

This aircraft joined the 17th BG on 18 November 1942, and was named and regularly flown by Capt William R Pritchard. He received a DFC for returning the badly damaged bomber from a mission to La Hencha on 1 March 1943. 41-17858 was the second 17th BG B-26 to reach the 50-mission mark, the first having been the 37th BS's *HELL CAT*. 1Lt Fred Meher flew this aircraft on its final mission, and Pritchard was on board as an observer. It is depicted here as it appeared just prior to returning to the US on 29 October 1943, having been repaired after sustaining battle damage on its last mission. By then the bomber had been credited with downing eight fighters and sinking three ships. The 34th BS Thunderbird emblem adorns the starboard side of the nose, and the B-26 sports propeller bosses painted in the squadron colour. Capt Pritchard flew *COUGHIN' COFFIN* home with a high-mission crew.

2

B-26B-40-MA 42-43311 B/N 09 *SPOT CASH!* of the 34th BS/17th BG, Villacidro, Sardinia, January 1944

42-43311 commenced operations with the 17th BG in September 1943, and the bomber went on to fly more than 140 missions until it was shot down on 26 April 1945 by Me 262s. Its nickname refers to money paid immediately upon delivery of goods or services, the meaning being rather more 'racier' when used in conjunction with a scantily clad nude! The radioman/waist gunner on the aircraft's final mission was SSgt Andrew T Poplos, who was killed. His brother Gust Poplos described what happened. 'On his 31st mission, Andrew's aeroplane *SPOT CASH!* was shot down over Neuberg an der Donau, near Gietlhausen. That day, the 17th BG was on its way to bomb Lechfeld airfield, but heavy cloud cover meant that most of the bombs were salvoed. At 1150 hrs, the formation had just turned northeast to return to Dijon when they were attacked by Me 262s from JV 44, led by Generalleutnant Adolf Galland. The 17th BG lost four aeroplanes, including two from the 34th BS. At 1150 hrs Galland had downed a B-26 for his 103rd victory, and on his second pass five minutes later, he fired at *SPOT CASH!*. With his first burst, he tore the side of the tail off up to the waist windows. Crippled by the jet's attack, the bomber nosed up and then fell off to the left into a spin, with smoke coming from both engines. In his upper turret gun position, Francis "Sid" Siddoway did not answer the co-pilot's inquiry of the crew's situation since his intercom had failed. Instead, he went to assist my brother, who had been wounded in the chest, just before the tail section broke away. Sid struggled to free the waist gun mount so that he could exit the aircraft through the waist

hatch. In the end, he was forced to push his feet through the window, and he slid out over the top of the gun. Moments after he had done this, the aeroplane went into a dive and the tail section broke off, taking tail gunner Sgt Richard K Smith with it. Smith managed to kick clear of the tail section and grab his parachute as the aeroplane was falling. He saw the bomber hit the ground and explode, and moments later he landed in a tree'.

3

B-26C-20-MO 41-35007 B/N 13 *Reddy Teddy* of the 34th BS/17th BG, Villacidro, Sardinia, January 1944

Reddy Teddy served with the 17th BG from August 1943 through to 24 January 1944, when it was retired after being declared war weary. The aeroplane's crew chief, TSgt Raymond I Linder, had the nose art and name faithfully reproduced on both sides of the bomber's nose. Beneath the pilot's window on the port side was the name 'Robby's Roost', Mississippi, and 'Colby's Corner', California appeared beneath the co-pilot's window on the starboard side. The legend 'Perk's Perch', NY, was carried on both sides of the nose just beneath the naked lady. Like *SPOT CASH!* before it, *Reddy Teddy* sports the full marking system then in use by the 17th BG.

4

B-26C-25-MO 41-35177 B/N 17 *UDEN UDEN'S OIL BURNER* of the 34th BS/17th BG, Villacidro, Sardinia, May 1944

41-35177 was in service with the 17th BG from 14 July 1943 through to 8 June 1944, when it was retired as war weary. The bomber was flown by 2Lts Robert R Bennett and co-pilot Tilman Beardon on their first combat mission, and they had named it after their instructor, 1Lt James Uden and his wife – Uden had been killed in a training accident. Bennett, Beardon and their crew had joined the 34th BS on 15 October 1943, and the officers were known as the 'Three Bs', referring to Bennett, Beardon and bombardier/navigator 2Lt William J Bell. The rest of the crew were SSgts Robert D Wilcox, William B O'Donovan and William Russell. The B-26's crew chief, TSgt Albert H Hurt, was aboard his beloved '177' when the left engine was shot out during an attack on the Rocca Secca bridge on 30 December 1943. Bennett later received a DFC for getting the bomber back home.

5

B-26C-45-MO 42-107729 B/N 17 *STUD DUCK* of the 34th BS/17th BG, Longvic, France, April 1945

STUD DUCK served with the 17th BG from 8 June 1944 until 24 April 1945, when it was shot down by an Me 262 from JV 44 over Schwabmünchen. The aeroplane's crew chief was originally TSgt Albert H Hurt, and its assigned pilot was Capt W D Lasly, whose name appears beneath the cockpit on the port side. The B-26's Battle Number and tail band have no edging, as the red stood out well enough on natural metal surfaces. The bomber has a replacement rudder, and therefore lacks the last four digits of its radio call number.

6
B-26B-2-MA 41-17903 *HELL CAT* of the 37th BS/17th BG, Djedeida, Tunisia, July 1943
HELL CAT was assigned to the 17th BG from 18 November 1942 through to 15 July 1943, although it may have flown with the 319th BG for a time during this period. The bomber's original pilot was Capt David B Taggart, and it was the first of the group's Marauders to complete 50 missions. *HELL CAT* was selected to return to the US with Capt B M Lloyd and his crew so that it could participate in a bond drive with the 319th BG's *Jabo/SKY KING the 2ND* and the 320th BG's *"LADY HALITOSIS"*. The bomber was duly replaced by B-26C-20 41-35159 B/N 35 *HELL CAT II*, which sported almost identical nose art. 41-17903 is depicted here as it would have looked upon its return to the US, having by then been credited with the destruction of nine fighters, three ships and two bridges. This early B-26 with the smaller flight surfaces also has the short-lived red surround to the national insignia that was authorised for use between 29 June and 14 August 1943.

7
B-26C-20-MO 41-35018 B/N 32 *Spooks* of the 37th BS/17th BG, Djedeida, Tunisia September 1943
Spooks was in service with the 17th BG from June 1943 until 16 March 1944. On the latter date, whilst being flown by 1Lt Chester M Angell, it was lost in a mid-air collision with B-26B-45 42-95782 B/N 26, flown by 2Lt C L Bosch. *Spooks* had near identical artwork applied to both sides of its nose, and it is seen here after completing ten missions – mission marks were only applied to the port side.

8
B-26C-45-MO 42-107768 B/N 35 *This is 'IT'* of the 37th BS/17th BG, Longvic, France, December 1944
42-107768 served from July 1944 until 24 December 1944, when it was shot down by Bf 109s whilst attempting to bomb the Messerschmitt aircraft factory at Frederickshafen. Its pilot that fateful day was 1Lt Fred M Abbott, and the aeroplane's crew chief was TSgt Kelley. *This Is 'IT'* was the second 17th BG Marauder to bear this name, having replaced B-26C-20 41-35140 B/N 35.

9
B-26B-40-MA 42-43278 B/N 36 *JERSEY BOUNCER III* of the 37th BS/17th BG, Villacidro, Sardinia, August 1944
JERSEY BOUNCER III was in service with the 17th BG from 12 September 1943 through to 17 December 1944, when it was shot down by flak whilst attacking defensive positions along the 'Siegfried Line' – its pilot on that day was 1Lt Donald V Leslie. On 2 July, 42-43278 had become the first B-26 from the 17th BG to complete 100 missions, and it had boosted its tally to 130 by the time of its demise. *JERSEY BOUNCER III* was unusual in that it sported artwork on both sides of its nose, as well as on both engine cowlings. On the port engine, a cartoon character accompanied the legend *UNDECIDED*, and a different character, with the legend *INDIFFERENT*, appeared on the starboard engine. The bomber is depicted here having completed 107 missions, with its port side nose art accompanied by renditions of three medals, including the DFC and Purple Heart.

10
B-26C-45-MO 42-107572 B/N 44 *Star-duster* of the 37th BS/17th BG, Villacidro, Sardinia, March 1944
Star-duster was in service from January 1944, and it was purportedly the first natural metal Marauder to be assigned to the 17th BG – Martin stopped camouflaging its B-26s when it commenced production of the B-55 and C-45 models. Crew chief TSgt Matlock named the bomber *Star-duster*, and once it had been prepared for combat, 37th BS CO Maj George Gibbons flew it on its first mission. *Star-duster* went on to complete 150 missions, and it also survived the war. A small rendition of a Vargas pin-up adorned the top of the artwork on the nose.

11
B-26B-40-MA 42-43308 B/N 68 *NEW YORK CENTRAL II* of the 95th BS/17th BG, Villacidro, Sardinia, July 1944
The first *NEW YORK CENTRAL* was one of the 17th BG's original Marauders (B-26B-2 41-17916), serving with the 34th BS until it was destroyed in a crash-landing following a mission to El Aouina on 24 February 1943. The bomber, like its replacement, was paid for by the employees of the New York Central Railroad. *NEW YORK CENTRAL II* entered service on 22 January 1944, and it had flown more than 100 missions by the time it was shot down by flak on 1 January 1945 whilst being piloted by 1Lt Joseph T Shoeps. The aeroplane is depicted here after completing 62 missions, when its assigned pilot was 1Lt R W Childers. His bombardier was 1Lt John D Venglar, whose name appears to the right of the Plexiglas nose.

12
B-26B-10-MA 41-18187 B/N 81 *"THE WOLVES"* of the 432nd BS/17th BG, Djedeida, Tunisia, October 1943
"THE WOLVES" saw service from April 1943 until it was shot down over Vieano, in Italy, whilst being flown by Capt Morris McCarver on 30 November 1943. It is depicted here after it had completed 35 missions. The aeroplane was adorned with the nicknames *"MOJO"*, *"REBEL"* and *"LIGHTNING"*, which referred to its pilot, co-pilot and bombardier. By the time the bomber was lost, it had completed 40 missions. 41-18187 was replaced by B-26B-45 42-95765 B/N 81, which was adorned with a similar name and nose art.

13

B-26B-30-MA 41-31962 B/N 86 *Old Iron Sides* of the 432nd BS/17th BG, Poretta, Corsica, October 1944

Old Iron Sides was the first B-26B-30-MA received by the 432nd BS in April 1943, and it survived to the end of war, flying a total of 175 missions. This model introduced bolt-on armour plating to protect the pilot, hence 41-31962's nickname.

14

B-26B-10-MA 41-18285 B/N 02 *Lady Katy* of the 437th BS/319th BG, Decimomannu, Sardinia, April 1944

Lady Katy is depicted here as it looked after completing 87 missions, and whilst assigned to pilot Flt Off Arthur W Cruse. A veteran of almost a year in frontline service, by the spring of 1944 it had been credited with the destruction of seven fighters and one naval vessel. The name adorned both sides of the nose, and this B-26 has the full complement of markings used by the 319th BG.

15

B-26C-11-MO 41-34868 B/N 04 *ZERO-4* of the 437th BS/319th BG, Decimomannu, Sardinia, June 1944

437th BS CO Maj John A Orb flew *ZERO-4* on its first mission in the autumn of 1943, and then participated in the bomber's 100th mission on 6 June 1944 as its co-pilot. The B-26 had completed 148 missions by the time it was flown back to the US by Capt Richard C Bushee in November 1944.

16

B-26C-45-MO 42-107550 B/N 08 *O'RILEY'S DAUGHTER* of the 437th BS/319th BG, Decimomannu, Sardinia, May 1944

42-107550 was delivered in natural metal finish, but had camouflage applied whilst in service with the 319th BG. This scheme differed from the 'official' version that the USAAF ordered its units to apply in the ETO due to the increased risk of attacks on airfields in France during late 1944. Field modification centres in the UK carried out the respraying for the aircraft assigned to the Ninth Air Force, although many of the brand new B-26Gs then arriving in-theatre had already been painted with a standardised version of the scheme prior to delivery. 42nd BW aircraft such as *O'RILEY'S DAUGHTER* had this darker shade of olive drab applied in the field. 42-107550 was also unusual in that it had neutral grey undersides. The bomber flew 110 missions with the 319th BG and was then transferred to the 320th BG, with whom it served out the war. By then it had flown 165 missions.

17

B-26C-11-MO 41-34914 B/N 18 *WILLIE Jr.* of the 437th BS/319th BG, Decimomannu, Sardinia, May 1944

WILLIE Jr. flew 61 missions before being retired from frontline operations and sent back to the US on 23 April 1944. Its crew chief, MSgt William Steele Jones Sr, adorned the aeroplane with the following legend prior to its departure; '*WILLIE Jr.* – This is, and has been, a God-dammed good aeroplane. He has completed 61 missions over Pantelleria, Sicily, Sardinia, Italy and France. He has seen his share of flak and fighters. He has been babied, nursed, cussed and blessed like most dammed women, so please, you people back where there is good whiskey and fine women, treat this aeroplane with the care he deserves. This aeroplane was named *WILLIE Jr.* after my son, William Steele Jones Jr, who was born at the same time we received this aeroplane – both are now house-broken.'

18

B-26C-15-MO 41-34938 B/N 35 *BIG ASS BIRD* of the 438th BS/319th BG, Decimomannu, Sardinia, June 1944

41-34938 was one of the first B-26s delivered to the 319th BG with the larger flight surfaces, hence its nickname. The Marauder reached the century mark when it led the group against German troop concentrations in the Albano and Ariccia areas on 1 June 1944, and went on to fly a total of 145 missions – the highest number for a bomber serving with the 319th BG.

19

B-26B-MA 41-17751 *"SNAFU"* of the 439th BS/319th BG, Horsham St Faith, Suffolk, November 1942

"SNAFU" (Situation Normal All Fucked Up) was one of a number of 319th BG Marauders that failed to complete the ferry flight to North Africa. It crashed into a hill near Huntington, in Yorkshire, in bad weather soon after the group had set off for Algeria on 12 November 1942. Pilot Capt Donald G Smith (a 'Doolittle Raider') and his crew perished. *SNAFU* is devoid of all makings, save for the nose art and radio call number on the fin. Smith's name appears beneath the pilot's window.

20

B-26B-15-MA 41-31609 *Jabo/SKY KING the 2ND* of the 439th BS/319th BG, Djedeida, Tunisia, July 1943

During July 1943, each of the three B-26 groups in the MTO were ordered to select a veteran Marauder and crew to return to the US for a special assignment. The 319th BG selected B-26C-15 41-34924 *Lovely Louise II* of the 439th BS and a crew led by Capt William F Erwin. Unfortunately, this aircraft sustained extensive flak damage during a mission to Messina on 14 July, so it was decided to send *Jabo/SKY KING the 2ND* instead. When the crews reported to Gen 'Hap' Arnold at the Pentagon, the men were told that they were to visit training fields to instill confidence in the B-26. At that time the USAAF was having trouble persuading men to fly the Marauder due to its tarnished reputation. The three crews divided up the bases to visit, with *Jabo/SKY KING the 2ND* touring airfields within the Southeast Training

Command. They also visited various locations to promote the purchase of war bonds. One of the crew's assignments was to visit an oil cracking plant at the request of the War Production Board so as to try to help settle a labour dispute. Before its departure to the US, *Jabo/SKY KING the 2ND* was suitably adorned with various logos such as *Gunner today, Goner tomorrow*, written beneath the top turret, as well as a list of the targets it had visited during its 37 missions – the aeroplane had also been credited with the destruction of eight fighters and two ships. The only unit marking applied to the bomber was its white tail band.

21
B-26C-11-MO 41-18326 B/N 52 *SKEETER* of the 439th BS/319th BG, Djedeida, Tunisia, July 1943

SKEETER is depicted here after it had completed 40 missions, by which time the bomber had also claimed two fighters. Note the aircraft's red and white DF loop, painted by its crew chief, TSgt Earl H Holtorp, so that he could easily recognise 41-18326 upon its return from a mission. Holtorp had also given the bomber its name, which was his favourite nickname for his wife. 41-18326 was lost on its 67th mission (on 21 January 1944) whilst being flown by 1Lt Clarice A Randall. It had an engine knocked out by flak over Orvieto and crashed minutes later – four parachutes were seen.

22
B-26C-11-MO 41-18303 B/N 60 *MISTLETOE* of the 439th BS/319th BG, Decimomannu, Sardinia, July 1944

MISTLETOE is depicted here as it appeared following its 100th mission, flown on 27 July 1944. The bomber's crew chief, TSgt Frank H Smigla, accompanied the crew on this operation, which saw the group bomb the railway bridge at Chivasso, in Italy. *MISTLETOE* went on to fly a further 18 missions with the 319th BG prior to its withdrawal from frontline operations.

23
B-26C-11-MO 41-18322 B/N 64 *Hell's Belle II* of the 439th BS/319th BG, Decimomannu, Sardinia, May 1944

Hell's Belle II was a replacement aeroplane for *Hell's Belle*, which had been one of the first 319th BG Marauders to see combat in North Africa. Written off in a force-landing in mid-1943, the aircraft was replaced by 41-18322. The latter bomber was initially assigned to 1Lt Jack H Logan and his crew. Upon the completion of their tour on Christmas Day 1943, the B-26 was assigned to 1Lt Elliot Lysco and his crew. On 1 May 1944, during a mission to the Campo di Marte railway marshalling yards in Florence, 41-18322 became the first USAAF bomber to complete 100 missions. A further 32 followed prior to its retirement.

24
B-26B-2-MA 41-17862 *"TIME'S AWASTIN"* of the 440th BS/319th BG, Labrador, October 1942

"TIME'S AWASTIN" never saw combat, as it was lost en route to the MTO. 1Lt Grover C Hodge Jr and his crew became lost in the winter weather, ran out of fuel and force-landed in Labrador on 10 October 1942. The B-26 and the remains of some of its crew were found the following March. Despite only being a few miles from an Eskimo village at Hebron, the crew was unsure of its location and awaited rescue. On 23 December three crewmen went for help and they were never seen again. Hodge's diary was found with his body, and it told of how the crew had starved to death – the last entry was dated 3 February 1943.

25
B-26B-15-MA 41-31590 B/N 79 *REPULSIVE RABBIT* of the 440th BS/319th BG, Serragia, Corsica, September 1944

REPULSIVE RABBIT completed its 100th mission on 5 September 1944. Unusually, this aeroplane had actually been renamed and received a new B/N mid way through its assignment to the 440th BS. Previously christened *Laura*, and carrying B/N 74 on its tail, *REPULSIVE RABBIT* is depicted here after reaching 120 missions – its pilot at the time was Capt William C 'Bill' Wood. The B-26 ultimately flew 125 missions with the 319th BG. The rabbit dressed in a German uniform, alluded to the unit's insignia, which depicted a rabbit sitting on a cloud dropping a bomb. The artwork appeared on both sides of the nose, but the name *REPULSIVE RABBIT* was on the right side only.

26
B-26C-11-MO 41-34892 B/N 83 *MODERN DESIGN* of the 440th BS/319th BG, Serragia, Corsica, September 1944

MODERN DESIGN was another of the 319th BG's B-26 centurions, the aircraft completing 104 missions prior to it being transferred to the 34th BS/17th BG in October 1944. The bomber's career had nearly been curtailed on 9 February 1944, however, when it was involved in a mid-air collision during a training flight. Nineteen-year-old pilot 2Lt Roscoe Nemer managed to land the bomber despite it having suffered considerable damage to its tailplane. The other Marauder involved in the incident (B-26B-15 41-31599 of the 438th BS, flown by 2Lt Charles W Erickson) crashed, and the only survivor of the three-man crew was dazed co-pilot 2Lt Maurice E Saunders.

27
B-26B-MA 41-17765 *"LADY HALITOSIS"* of the 441st BS/320th BG, Massicault, Tunisia, July 1943

"LADY HALITOSIS" was one of the 320th BG's original Marauders, and after having flown 43 missions it was selected to return to the US (see profile 20 for details). A selected crew led by pilot 1Lt William Van Marter flew the aeroplane home on 15 July 1943. By that time it had been credited with the destruction of six fighters and three ships. The artwork appeared on both sides of the bomber's nose, and the starboard side also

sported an early example of the 441st BS insignia. The unit applied this marking to most of its B-26s, and there were three distinct versions of the design. 41-17765 also had an astrodome atop the fuselage, which was a standard fitment for B-26 lead ships – the mission commander viewed his formation from this position.

28

B-26C-20-MO 41-35070 *FRANCES JOAN* B/N 04 of the 441st BS/320th BG, El Bathan, Tunisia, October 1943

41-35070 is depicted here after completing 15 missions, and it sports the second version of the 441st BS insignia. This aircraft was hit by flak and crashed near Viterbo, in Italy, on 21 January 1944. Some 64 years later, the bomber's pilot, 1Lt Louis Valls, was posthumously awarded the DFC, which was presented to his family on 28 March 2008. The citation accompanying the award read, in part, '1Lt Valls led his crew as the deputy leader of his flight, and deputy leader of a 17-aeroplane formation, against the heavily defended railway bridge southeast of Orvieto, in Italy. His aircraft was struck by heavy anti-aircraft fire early on the bomb run, causing it to catch fire, and heavy smoke entered the aeroplane through the open bomb-bay doors. With the aircraft fatally crippled, the crew was instructed to bale out, despite imminent danger of the bombs exploding. 1Lt Valls realised the importance of the mission, and dependence of the formation on his aircraft for a successful attack. Displaying great courage and superior flying ability, he held the aircraft in formation and continued the bomb run. Just after 1Lt Valls' crew released their bombs, the aircraft received a second devastating direct flak strike on the left engine, forcing the B-26 into a steep bank toward the ground. Maintaining the controls long enough to allow two crew members to parachute to safety, 1Lt Valls, his co-pilot, navigator, bombardier and top-turret gunner all perished, but not before they inflicted heavy damage to a key railway bridge.'

29

B-26B-50-MA 42-96016 B/N 04 *Doris K./Iidalizeya* of the 441st BS/320th BG, Decimomannu, Sardinia, May 1944

42-96016 was the regular mount of Capt Sidney 'Snuffy' Smith, CO of the 441st BS from 27 July 1944 through to 12 March 1945. The aeroplane was named after Smith's wife, Doris, and was also adorned with her picture. *Doris K./Iidalizeya* flew well over 100 missions, and survived the war. The Marauder has the factory-painted medium green scallops applied to its tail section – a common feature found on many B-26B-50/55 models. These were in addition to the areas of medium green on the nose and fuselage sides that was also common to earlier models of the Marauder.

30

B-26B-45-MA 42-95753 B/N 08 *MY-GAL* of the 441st BS/320th BG, Alto, Corsica, September 1944

MY-GAL was formerly named *TABOO*, and the remnants of this name are discernable beneath the more recent nose art. 42-95753 was flown on its 100th mission by 1Lt Scott and his crew on 19 October 1944, when the group attacked the Ossenigo railway cutting on 19 October 1944. The B-26 was subsequently lost on 23 December when on its 115th mission. Manned by 2Lt Richard Dickey and his crew, and sent to bomb the Breisach bridge, *MY-GAL* suffered a direct flak hit in the bomb-bay and broke in two – there were no survivors.

31

B-26B-10-MA 41-18305 B/N 14 *Miss Manchester* of the 441st BS/320th BG, Decimomannu, Sardinia, December 1943

Depicted here after 38 missions, *Miss Manchester* sports the early style white battle number that would have later been changed to yellow during January 1944. On 21 January *Miss Manchester* was brought down by flak over Orvieto. Its pilot, 1Lt Robert B Currie, was awarded the DFC for holding the burning aeroplane level long enough for his crew to bale out – five parachutes were seen before the bomber exploded. *Miss Manchester* was replaced by B-26B-50 42-95884 B/N 14 *Miss Manchester*, which flew 100+ missions and survived the war.

32

B-26G-5-MA 43-34284 B/N 32 *Green Eyed Glodine* of the 442nd BS/320th BG, Longvic, France, January 1945

Green Eyed Glodine was named by its regular pilot, 1Lt Robert A Perrine, in honour of his wife, Glodine. F/G-model Marauders were a big improvement over earlier versions of the bomber, with their primary design change being a 3.5-degree increase to the wing incidence. Despite a slight decrease in speed, this change gave a shorter take-off run and better handling that would have saved the lives of many previous crews. The shorter take-off run initially took pilots by surprise when the 320th BG launched its multi-ship take-offs from Decimomannu, as G-models got airborne much quicker than their previous B-26B/Cs.

33

B-26C-20-MO 41-34999 B/N 33 *"SHIF'LESS"* of the 442nd BS/320th BG, Decimomannu, Sardinia, February 1944

"SHIF'LESS" is depicted here after reaching the 75-mission mark in early 1944, by which time its crews had claimed the destruction of three enemy fighters. The aeroplane sports a version of the 'running duck' insignia that the 442nd BS applied to many of its bombers. On 18 December 1943, 1Lt Richard A Dodelin flew 41-34999 to the Antheor railway viaduct, and during the course of its bomb run, an 88 mm flak shell exploded nearby and mortally wounded top turret gunner SSgt Wesley D Dolan. Engineer/waist gunner SSgt Joseph Garbenches was later awarded the DFC for aiding

Dolan and then manning his turret, despite having been wounded by shrapnel from the same flak shell.

34
B-26B-4-MA 41-18023 B/N 55 *Boomerang* of the 443rd BS/320th BG, El Bathan, Tunisia, September 1943

Boomerang was the aeroplane from which the 320th BG derived its nickname. The B-26's markings are unusual for the 320th BG, as its serial number has been re-applied over the early white battle number, and there is no yellow tail band. *Boomerang* also sports the radio call letter 'C', this marking system being the first method of individual aeroplane identification to be used by B-26 squadrons. *Boomerang* is depicted here after completing 53 missions, and having downed two enemy fighters. Some of the mission markings have a small red 'V' painted on them, but to date the significance of this embellishment remains unknown. Each member of the crew had their nickname painted on the fuselage of the aircraft in their respective positions. The legend *'FEAGIN the VIPER'* appears beneath the pilot's window for pilot 1Lt L W Feagin, and the name beneath the tail gunner's position reads *'NOAK'S NOOK'*, in honour of tail gunner Sgt Merrill 'Shorty' Noakes. Other crew names applied to the aeroplane were *'SPIKE'S SPOT'* for co-pilot 2Lt Cloyd T Pearce, *'PACE'S PATIO'* for bombardier 2Lt Lemuel Max Pace, *'BERNIE'S BEANERY'* for radio-gunner Sgt N Bernstein and *'GAMBLE'S GADGET'* for turret gunner Sgt Warren E Gamble.

35
B-26B-10-MA 41-18288 B/N 62 *Scramboogie* of the 443rd BS/320th BG, Decimomannu, Sardinia, January 1944

Scramboogie is seen here after completing 40 missions. Although the nickname of the bomber was not written on its nose, the Marauder was adorned with a reclining pin-up and the 443rd BS insignia. Photographs show that a least two versions of this badge were applied to many of the squadron's longer-lived aeroplanes.

36
B-26B-MA 41-17724 *RED HOT!* of the 444th BS/320th BG, Montiescquieu, Algeria, June 1943

RED HOT! is depicted here as it appeared following a crash-landing at Montiescquieu on 15 June 1943. Pilot 1Lt John B Stumm made a force-landing that wrecked the Marauder after it had sustained battle damage during an attack on Milo airfield. The name of the aircraft's assigned pilot, 1Lt Don M Towns, appears beneath the pilot's window, and the unit's 'rabbit' emblem adorns its nose. Many of the squadron's early Marauders sported this nose art, as it was representative of the 444th BS insignia. *RED HOT!'s* national insignia also sports a yellow surround, this being a short-lived aid for ground-to-air recognition purposes during Operation *Torch*.

37
B-26B-3-MA 41-17959 *Miss Fortune* of the 444th BS/320th BG, Montiescquieu, Algeria, June 1943

Miss Fortune, flown by Capt Theodore M Dorman, led the 320th BG's first bombing mission against a land-based target – Carloforte harbour, on Sardinia – on 22 April 1943. It is depicted here after completing 18 missions, and Dorman's name appears below the pilot's window. Almost identical artwork was applied to the starboard side of the bomber's nose.

38
B-26C-45-MO 42-107752 B/N 88 *MISS. Arkansas* of the 444th BS/320th BG, Decimomannu, Sardinia, August 1944

One of the more famous Marauders to serve with the 320th BG, this aircraft's notoriety almost certainly stemmed from its elaborate artwork, which was applied to both sides of the bomber's nose. There are are slight differences between the two versions, and the name appeared on the starboard side only. The nose art incorporated the distinctive sharksmouth that adorned the majority of the aeroplanes assigned to the 444th BS from mid-1944 onwards. The sharksmouth effectively replaced the earlier rabbit artwork as a squadron identification marking.

39
B-26C-45-MO 42-107825 B/N 98 *Ol' Folks* of the 444th BS/320th BG, Longvic, France, December 1944

Ol' Folks was another ex-319th BG Marauder that had had olive drab paint applied to its uppersurfaces by its former owner. 42-107825 had been *Sweet Lew's Baby* (B/N 55) when serving with the 439th BS. For a time, *Ol' Folks* retained the latter unit's yellow cowling rings, despite having being reassigned to the 320th BG. The field-applied camouflage has an almost straight mid-fuselage demarcation, and avoids both the data block and the radio call number on the fin. The latter remains in its original black – it would have been yellow if the camouflage had been factory-applied.

Back Cover
B-26G-1-MA 43-34192 B/N 38 *Suzy Mae* of the 442nd BS/320th BG, Longvic, France, November 1944

Suzy Mae is depicted here in standard late war factory-applied olive drab camouflage. The bomber was transferred from a Ninth Air Force B-26 group to the 320th BG in late 1944, at which point it had its D-Day invasion stripes removed. A section of its wing camouflage was also stripped off in the process. The port engine bore the name *Norma* applied in the same style as the aeroplane's name. This particular G-model had the lower Plexiglas section of its Bell tail turret replaced with a canvas covering, and blast deflectors were also fitted forward of the waist gun positions.

INDEX

References to illustrations are shown in **bold**.
Plates are shown with page and caption
locators in brackets.